A

ANAL......

OF

BLACKSTONE'S COMMENTARIES

ON

𝕿𝖍𝖊 𝕷𝖆𝖜𝖘 𝖔𝖋 𝕰𝖓𝖌𝖑𝖆𝖓𝖉,

IN A

SERIES OF QUESTIONS,

TO WHICH THE STUDENT IS TO FRAME HIS OWN ANSWERS, BY READING THAT WORK.

⚫⚫⚫

By BARRON FIELD, Esq.

OF THE INNER TEMPLE, BARRISTER AT LAW.

⚫⚫⚫

His explicatis, fons legum et juris invenire potest.
CICERO, de Legibus lib. i.

Σχεδον γαρ τουτο ἡμιν ὑπερ ἁπαντων των νομων καλλιςον τε και αριςον προοιμιον.
PLATO de Legibus. lib. x.

◆

FIRST AMERICAN FROM THE SECOND LONDON EDITION

◆

NEW-YORK:

PUBLISHED BY STEPHEN GOULD,

LAW BOOKSELLER, (SIGN OF LORD COKE,)

Corner of Wall and Broad Streets.

William Grattan, Printer.

1822.

TO

THE RIGHT HONOURABLE

EDWARD LORD ELLENBOROUGH,

&c. &c. &c.

LORD CHIEF JUSTICE OF ENGLAND.

THIS HUMBLE COMPILATION

IS, WITH HIS LORDSHIP'S PERMISSION,

MOST RESPECTFULLY INSCRIBED,

BY

HIS VERY OBEDIENT

AND OBLIGED SERVANT,

BARRON FIELD.

INNER TEMPLE,
14th Jan. 1811

PREFACE.

TILL the publication of Blackstone's Commentaries, the Law-Student entered upon his long and difficult voyage almost without rudder or compass. Every other science had its elementary books, its maps and its charts; and the course of its study was plainly marked out. In the Law alone, the most complex of sciences, the Student had to find out not only what he had to learn, but where that learning was contained. Every body, who is at all conversant with books, is aware that the next advantage to an acquaintance with any particular subject, is to know where that acquaintance may be formed. "Knowledge," said Dr. Johnson to Mr. Cambridge, who asked him to account for a propensity to look at the backs of books, "is of two kinds; we know a subject ourselves, or we know where we can find information upon it. When we enquire into any subject, the first thing we have to do, is to know what books have treated of it:" and this principle is well applied by the Doctor, in his life of Edmund Smith, to Gilbert Walmsley; these are the words: "His acquaintance with books was great; and what he did not immediately know, he could at least tell

where to find." Sir William Blackstone has fur-
nished every Law-Student with this first step to
knowledge; and if his Commentaries may sometimes evince too servile a compliance with things
as they are, yet it is now too late in the day to
undervalue their general excellence and utility.
To the Law-Student they are already a sort of
Bible; and it will, therefore, excite in him little
surprise, that the compiler of the following pages
has founded a Catechism upon them. He be-
lieves, that few Students have read Blackstone's
Commentaries without a pen in their hand; and
this is the way, in which, for his own improve-
ment, he chose to employ *his* pen. Analyses of
Blackstone's Commentaries there doubtless are
many in manuscript; and Mr. Gibbon tells us,
that "a copious and critical abstract of that work
was his first serious production in his native lan-
guage." Indeed there seems to be scarcely any
better aid to the memory, than that of analysis.
It divests each point of all that accompanying observation, which, while it intends to illustrate,
frequently obscures and perplexes the subject,
and, by thus reducing every topic to a simple
disposeable shape, it assists the mind in what may
be considered as its most useful operation in every
science, the arrangement of ideas. For it is by
arrangement alone, that the place of each idea
becomes familiar and certain to us, and that we
are enabled to receive from it a firm and lasting

impression. It is rather astonishing, therefore, that no analysis of Blackstone has ever been published,—the little work under that title, with which Sir William Blackstone himself preceded his Commentaries, being intended merely "to exhibit their order and principle divisions" (these are the Commentator's own words), as a syllabus of the course of Lectures in which they were originally submitted to the University of Oxford, and being wholly undeserving of the name of an analysis. The following pages are intended to supply this *desideratum*, and that in a way which will promote the student's industry, rather than render it superfluous; for the questions here put, will force every student, by making him frame his own answers to them, to analyse Blackstone's Commentaries for himself, and will, at the same time, afford the surest test, that he has read them with proper attention.

The plan, upon which the following compilation is founded, has long been tried with success in studying the elements of languages, and the profession of divinity. The first work of the same nature, with which the present writer is acquainted, is Dr. Priestley's " Scripture Catechism, or a Series of Questions, with references to the Scriptures instead of Answers," a publication which was followed by " A Series of Questions, comprising the History of the four Gospels, and the Acts of the Apostles," upon the same plan.

by an uncle of the present writer. He is in-
formed, however, that even before Dr. Priestley's
publication, Mrs. Barbauld was in the habit of
instructing her pupils by this method ; and they
both may have received the idea of it from the col-
lections of problems, which are usually proposed
for solution in books of science. Mr. Morgan's
Grammaticæ Quæstiones, upon the same plan, applied to the Eton Latin Grammar, are well known
in schools ; and Mr. Bradley has adopted a similar
method of facilitating the pupil's acquaintance with
the Latin Grammar of Dr. Valpy, and the English
one of Lindley Murray. Attached to Mr. Joyce's
Scientific Dialogues and Conversations in Che-
mistry, there are also questions without answers.

The compiler recommends the student to apply
himself, after reading each chapter of Blackstone's
Commentaries, to the corresponding chapter of
the following questions, and to set down his answers to them in writing. "The science of law,"
says Sir William Jones, " is so complex that without writing, which is the chain of memory, it is
impossible to remember a thousandth part of what
we read or hear."

The compiler has made use of Sir William
Blackstone's own words, wherever he was able to
do so, and has endeavoured, as much as possible,
to prevent a succeeding question from answering
a preceding ; but to effect this was sometimes im-
practicable, and the Student, who really wishes

to trust his own memory, will do well always to answer a first question, before he look at a second.

It is presumed by the compiler, that in those *schools*, where Blackstone's Commentaries are read, (and what schoolboy might not profitably devote half the time allotted to the *making* of Latin verses, to at least the 1st and 4th volumes of the Commentator ?) the following questions will perform the greatest services of which they are capable.

INNER TEMPLE,
20th September, 1810.

THE figures at the end of each question refer to the pages of Blackstone (and those of all the editions are alike) where its answer may be found. It was unnecessary to note the Volume, as it is well known that the four Books of Blackstone correspond with the four Volumes.

INTRODUCTION.

SECTION II.

Of the Nature of Laws in general.

1. WHAT is *law*, in its most general and comprehensive sense? 38.
2. What is *law*, in its more confined sense, and that in which it is the present *commentator's* business to consider it? 39.
3. What is the *law of Nature*? 39.
4. To what one *precept*, may the *law of nature* be reduced? 41.
5. Has God revealed any portions of this *law* to us? 42.
6. Upon what two foundations depend all human laws? 42.
7. As the whole race of mankind form separate states, is there not a third kind of *law*? 43.
8. What is that *law* called, by which particular nations are governed? 44.
9. How does the *commentator* define that *law*? 44.
10. What three *forms of government* are there? 49.

11. What peculiar quality does each of these *forms of government* possess ; and what effect have these several qualities upon the *laws* of their respective *governments?* 49, 50.

12. What is the nature of the British *form of government?* 50, 51.

13. With whom lies the right to make *laws,* in every *government?* 52.

14. Of what four parts may every *law* be said to consist ? 53, 54.

15 Wherein consists the difference between those *things prohibited* by the *law,* which are *mala in se,* and those which are *mala prohibita?* 54, 55. 57, 58.

16. What five helps are there to the interpretation of *laws* ? 59.

17. How is *equity* defined by Grotius ? 62.

SEC. III.

Of the Laws of England.

1. INTO what two kinds may the *municipal law* of England be divided ? 63.

2. What does the first of these kinds of *law* include ? 63.

3. Where is it to be found ? 63, 64.

4. Of what degree of antiquity must its *maxims* and *customs* be, to entitle them to validity ? 67.

5. Into what three kinds is it distinguishable ? 67.

6. How are its *customs* or *maxims* to be known; and by whom is their validity to be determined?   69.

7. What is the doctrine of the *law*, as to *following precedents?*   70.

8. What three things do the rules relating to *particular customs* regard?   75.

9. Wherein do the *customs* of London differ from all others in point of *trial?*   76.

10. What are the seven necessary requisites to make a *custom* good?   77, 78.

11. To what, however, must all *special customs* submit?   79.

12. What are understood by those *peculiar laws*, which, by *custom*, are adopted and used only in certain *peculiar courts*, and jurisdictions?   79.

13. What is understood by each of these laws, absolutely taken?   80, 82.

14. What are the four species of *courts*, in which these *laws* are permitted to be used?   83.

15. Under what superintendency, are all these courts?   84.

16. To whom does an appeal from them lie, in the last resort?   84.

17. Of what does the second kind of *municipal law* consist?   85.

18. Into what four kinds is it distinguishable 85, 86.

19. What two connexions has it with the first kind of *municipal law?*   86.

20. What are the ten principal rules to be observed with regard to the construction of the second kind of *municipal law?*   87—91.

21. For what purpose are our *courts of equity* established ; and in what matters only are they conversant ?   92.

SEC. IV.

Of the Countries subject to the Laws of England.

1. WHAT does the *kingdom of England,* by the *common law*, include ?   93.

2. How is *Wales* governed ; and in what particuculars does it differ from the kingdom of *England?*   93—95.

3. How is *Scotland* governed ; and what four observations are to be made upon the *articles* and *act of union* between *England* and *Scotland?*   95—98.

4. How is the *town* of *Berwick-upon-Tweed* governed ; what *writs* run there ; and by whom may all local matters arising there be tried ?   99.

5. How is *Ireland* governed ? 100—104. And see Mr. Justice Christian's note (14) to this chapter.   104.

6. How are the Isles of *Wight, Portland, Thanet,* &c. governed ?   105.

7. How is the Isle of *Man* governed ? 105, 106.

8. How are the Isles of *Jersey, Guernsey, Sark, Alderney*, and their appendages, governed ? 106.

9. How are our *Plantations abroad* governed ? 107, 108.

10. Of what three sorts are our *Colonies*, with respect to their internal polity ; what is the form of *government* in most of them ; and what is declared, as to the laws of *plantations*, by statute 7 & 8 W. III. c. 22., and as to the subordination of the *American plantations*, by statute 6 Geo. III. c. 12 ?   108, 109.

11. But what was the *King* empowered to do by statute 22 Geo. III. c. 46. ; and what does he acknowledge by the first article of the *definitive treaty* of *peace* and friendship between His *Britannic Majesty* and the *United States of America* ? To be answered from Mr. Justice Christian's note (17) to this chapter.   109.

12. How are any *foreign dominions*, which may belong to the *King* by *hereditary descent*, by *purchase*, or other acquisition, governed ? 109, 110.

13. What part of the *sea* is subject to the *common law*, and what part to the jurisdiction of our *Courts of Admiralty?*   110.

14. To what two divisions is the *territory* of *England* liable ?   110.

15. How is the first division subdivided ?   111.

16. What is a *parish:* how were the boundaries of *parishes* originally ascertained : how is the

frequent intermixture of *parishes* one with another to be accounted for; how are some *lands extra parochial;* to whom are their *tithes* payable; yet what does the statute 17 Geo. II. c. 37. enact as to *extra-parochial* waste and marsh *lands,* when improved and drained? 111—113.

17 How is the second division subdivided? 114.

18. What was a *tithing?* 114.

19. What is a *town* now, what a *city,* and what a *borough?* 114, 115.

20. What is a *hundred,* what a *wapentake,* what a *county* or *shire,* what a *lathe,* what a *rape,* and what a *trithing?* 115, 116.

21. What is a *county-palatine;* what three *counties* are now of this nature; whence is the origin of their privileges; how were the powers of their owners abridged in 27 Hen. VIII.; and who are those owners now? 116—119.

22. What is the *Isle of Ely?* 119.

23. What is a *county-corporate?* 120.

COMMENTARIES

ON THE

LAWS OF ENGLAND.

BOOK THE FIRST.

OF THE RIGHTS OF PERSONS.

CHAPTER I.

Of the absolute Rights of Individuals.

1. WHAT are the two primary and principal *objects* of the laws of England? 122.
2. How is the first of these *objects* subdivided? 122.
3. How is the second of these *objects* subdivided? 122.
4. Of what two sorts are those *rights of persons,* which are commanded to be observed by the *municipal law?* 123.
5. How are *persons* divided by the law? 123.
6. Of what two sorts are the *rights of persons* considered in their first, or natural capacity? 123.

7. What does the law say, as to the *absolute duties* of man? 124.
8. What is *political* or *civil liberty?* 125.
9. How is *political* or *civil liberty* distinguished from *natural liberty?* 125.
10. How have the *absolute rights* of Englishmen been asserted in parliament? 127, 128.
11. To what three principal or primary articles may these *rights* be reduced? 129.
12. In what does the first consist? 129.
13. How is an *infant, in ventre sa mere,* considered by the law? 130.
14. What does the law mean by *duress per minas?* 131.
15. What is the distinction between a *civil* and a *natural death?* 132.
16. What does *magna carta* say as to the personal security of a " *liber homo ;*" and what is enacted to the same effect by statutes 5 Edw. III. c. 9. and 28 Edw. III. c. 3.? 133, 134.
17. In what does the second *absolute right* of Englishmen consist? 134.
18. What is a writ of *habeas corpus,* and when may it be sued out? 135.
19. What does the law mean by *duress of imprisonment?* 136.
20· What is necessary to make an *imprisonment* lawful; and when is the *gaoler* not bound to detain the *prisoner?* 137.
21. Can an Englishman be restrained from leaving the kingdom? 137.

22. Can he be compelled to leave it? 137.

23. In what does the third *absolute right* of Englishmen consist? 138.

24. In case it would be beneficial to the public that a new road should be made through the grounds of a private person, how will the legislature compel that person to acquiesce in its being made? 139.

25. What *taxes* only can a *subject* of *England* be constrained to pay? 140.

26. What are the five secondary and subordinate *absolute rights* of Englishmen? 141—143.

27. What does *magna carta* say as to the right of every *Englishman* to apply to the *courts* of *justice* for redress of *injuries;* and what is enacted to the same effect by statutes 2 Edw. III. c. 8. and 11 Ric. II. c. 10. ; and what is declared by statutes 1 W. & M. st. 2. c. 2. and 16 Car. I. c. 10. (upon the dissolution of the *Star-Chamber*)? 141, 142.

28. To prevent any riot or tumult, under the pretence of petitioning for the redress of grievances, what is provided by statute 13 Car. II. st. 1. c. 5. ; but, under these regulations, what is declared by the same statute 1 W. & M. ? 143.

29. What is declared by the same statute, as to the right of every *subject* to have *arms* for his defence? 144.

CHAP. II.

Of the Parliament.

15. What are the disqualifications of a *member of parliament?*   162.

16. From what one maxim has the whole of the *law and custom of parliament* its original?   163.

17. Of what extent are the *privileges of parliament?*   164.

18. What are some of the more notorious *privileges* of either house of *parliament?*   164— 167.

19. What are the peculiar *privileges* of the *house of lords?*   167, 168.

20. What are the peculiar *privileges* of the *house of commons?*   169, 170.

21. What are the qualifications of *electors* of *knights of the shire?*   172, 173.

22. What are the qualifications of *electors* of *citizens* and *burgesses?*   174, 175.

23. What are the qualifications of persons to be *elected members* of the *house of commons?* 175, 176.

24. What is the method of proceeding in regard to *elections,* both of *knights of the shire* and of *members for cities and boroughs?*   177, 178, 180.

25. What measures are taken at *elections* to prevent all undue influence upon the *electors;* and what if any *revenue officer* intermeddle in *elections?*   178, 179.

26. What is enacted to prevent *bribery* and *corruption* at *elections* ? 179.

27. What if the *returning officer* do not return such *members* only as are duly elected ? 180.

28. What is the method of making *laws?* 181 —185.

29. In what two ways may the *royal assent* to a *bill* be given ? 184, 185.

30. Whom hath an *act of parliament* power to bind : how only can it be altered, amended, dispensed with, suspended, or repealed ; and what is declared by the statute 1 W. & M. st. 2. c. 2. as to regal authority over *laws ?* 185, 186.

31 What is an *adjournment* of the *houses of parliament?* 186.

32. What is a *prorogation* of the *houses of parliament?* 187.

33. What is a *dissolution* of the *houses of parliament ?* 187.

34. In what three ways may this *dissolution* be effected ? 187—189.

35. But the calling a new *parliament* immediately on the inauguration of a *successor* to the *crown* being found inconvenient, and dangers being apprehended from having no *parliament* in being, in case of a disputed succession, what was enacted by statutes 7 & 8 W. III. c. 15. and 6 Ann. c. 7 ? 188.

36. What is the extent of time that the same *parliament* is allowed to sit, by the statute 1 Geo. I. st. 2. c. 38. ? 189.

———

CHAP. III.

Of the King and his Title.

1. IN whom is the supreme *executive power* of this kingdom lodged ? 190.
2. Under what six distinct views may the *royal person* be considered ? 190.
3. What is the grand fundamental maxim upon which the *jus coronæ*, or right of succession to the *throne* of these kingdoms depends? 191.
4. Does the descent of the *crown* correspond with the feodal path of descents, chalked out by the *common law* in the succession to *landed estates.* 193, 194.
5. Does the doctrine of *hereditary* right imply an *indefeasible* right to the *throne* ? 195.
6. The *crown* being capable of being limited or transferred, does it not lose its decendible quality ? 196.
7. What *kings* have been successively constituted the *common stocks*, or *ancestors* of the English descent ? 197—217.

8. What did the *convention of estates*, or representative body of the nation, declare at the
   revolution ?   211.
9. And how did they settle the succession to the
   throne ?   214.
10. On the impending failure of the protestant
    line of Charles I. (whereby the *throne* might
    again have become vacant), to whom did
    the King and parliament extend the settle-
    ment of the *crown ?*   216.

CHAP. IV.

Of the King's Royal Family.

1. WHAT is the first and most considerable
   branch of the King's *royal family*, regarded
   by the laws of England ?   218.
2. What are the three kinds of *queens ?*   218
3. What are the powers, prerogatives, rights,
   dignities, and duties of the first kind of
   queen?   218, 222.
4. What are the prerogatives of the second kind
   of *queen* above other women ?   218, 219.
5. In what does her *revenue* consist ?   219—222.
6. What are the privileges of the third kind of
   queen ?   223.

7. How are the *Prince of Wales* or *heir apparent* to the *crown*, and his *royal consort*, and the *Princess royal*, or eldest daughter of the King, regarded by the laws ? 223.

8. How are the rest of the *royal family* regarded by the laws ? 224—226.

9. Does the law make any distinction between the King's *children* and his *grand children* ? 225.

10. What is enacted by statute 12 Geo. III. c. 11. as to the capability of the decendants of the body of King George II. to contract *matrimony* ? 226.

CHAP. V.

Of the Councils belonging to the King.

1. What are the four *councils*, which the law has assigned to advise with the *King* ? 227—230.

2. By whom are *privy counsellors* created ? 230.

3. What are the qualifications of a *privy counsellor* ? 230.

4. What are the duties of a *privy counsellor* ? 230, 231.

5. What is the power of the *privy council* ? 231, 232.

6. What are the privileges of a *privy counsellor?*
232.

7. How may the *privy council* be dissolved, and
what is enacted as to its dissolution, by
statute 6 Ann. c. 7. ?   232.

CHAP. VI.

Of the King's Duties.

1. What are the principal duties of the *King*,
and what is expressly declared, on this subject, by statute 12 & 13 W. Ill. c. 2. ? 233,
234. 236.

2. By what contract is he bound to execute these
duties ?   235.

3. Upon what principle is the duty of protection
impliedly as much incumbent upon the *Sove-
reign* before coronation as after ?   236.

4. With respect to the *King's* duty to maintain
the established *religion*, what is done by the
act of union, 5. Ann. c. 8. ?   236.

CHAP. VII.

Of the King's prerogative.

1. WHAT is usually understood by the word
prerogative?   239.

2. What are the two species of *prerogative*, and how are they defined ? 239, 240.

3. Into what three kinds may the first species of *prerogative* be divided ? 240.

4. What is the first attribute the law ascribes to the *King*, in which his *dignity* consists ? 241.

5. What is the difference between a *king* and an *emperor* ? 242.

6. What remedy have the subjects of England, in case the *crown* should invade their rights by *private injury* ? 243.

7. What remedy have they, in case of such invasion by *public oppression* ? 244.

8. Should any *King* endeavour to subvert the constitution, by breaking the original contract between him and the people, violate the fundamental laws, and withdraw himself out of the kingdom, to what would this conjunction of circumstances amount ? 245.

9. What is the second legal attribute in which the *King's dignity* consists ? 245.

10. What is the meaning of that attribute ? 246.

11. What else does the law determine, in pursuance of this principle ? 247, 248.

12. What is the third legal attribute of the *King's dignity* ? 249.

13. In what does the *King's authority* consist ? 250.

14. How has Locke defined *prerogative* ? 252.

15. What are the *King's* five principal *rights* or *prerogatives*, as representative of the people

with regard to foreign concerns? 253. 257
—259.

16. How are the rights, powers, duties, and privileges of *ambassadors* determined? 253.

17. What are some of these privileges? 253, 254, 256.

18. When are *letters of marque* and *reprisal* granted? 258.

19. What does *magna carta* declare respecting foreign merchants? 260.

20. What are the *King's* six rights or prerogatives, and in what six characters is he considered, in domestic affairs? 261, 262. 266. 271. 273. 279.

21. What five powers has the *King*, considered as *generalissimo* within the kingdom? 262—265.

22. What, by statute 4 Hen. IV. c. 20., is the penalty for landing elsewhere than at the *"great ports"* of the *sea?* 264.

33. Who, by statute 8 Eliz. c. 13., are empowered to set up *beacons* or *sea-marks;* and what is the penalty for taking down any known *sea-mark?* 265.

24. If the *King* by *writ* of *ne exeat regnum*, prohibit a man from going abroad, or if the *King* send him a *writ* when abroad commanding his return, what is the penalty of disobedience in either case? 266.

25. To whom have our *kings* delegated their whole judicial power; and what is enacted

in order to maintain the dignity and inde-
pendence of the *judges* in the *superior
courts*, by statutes 13 W. III. c. 2. and
1 Geo. III. c. 23.?   267, 268.

26. Why would it be a still higher absurdity if
the *King* sat in *judgment* in *criminal prosecutions?*   268.

27. Whence arises the *King's prerogative* of pardoning *offences?*   268, 269.

28. What is the legal *ubiquity* of the *King*, and
what follows thence?   270.

29. What force have the *King's proclamations?*
270.

30. Under what three articles will the *King's
prerogative*, so far as it relates to domestic
commerce, fall?   274. 276.

31. What three rights arise to the *King*, as the
head and supreme governor of the national
church?   279, 280.

32. Of what does the *convocation*, or *ecclesiastical
synod*, in England, consist?   279, 280.

CHAP. VIII.

Of the King's Revenue.

1. OF what two kinds is the *King's revenue?* 281.
2. Of what two natures is the first of these kinds
of *revenue?*   281.

3. What *revenue* does the *King* derive from his *bishopricks?* 282.

4. To what is the *King* entitled of every *bishop?* 283.

5. To what *tithes* is the *King* entitled? 283, 284.

6. To what portion of all the *spiritual preferments* in the kingdom is the *King* entitled? 284.

7. What is meant by *Queen Anne's bounty?* 286.

8. Of what lands does the *crown* receive the rents and profits? 286.

9. How have the grants and leases of these lands been regulated by *act of parliament?* 286, 287.

10. Do any advantages arise to the *King* from *military tenures?* 287.

11. What was the *prerogative* of *purveyance* and *pre-emption;* and for what branch of *revenue* did what *King* exchange it? 287, 288.

12. What *revenue* did and does the *King* derive from *wine-licences?* 288.

13. Do any profits arise to the *King* from his *forests?* 289.

14. What *revenue* does the *King* derive from his ordinary *courts of justice,* and what is enacted by statute 1 Ann. st. l. c. 7., as to all future grants of their profits? 289, 290.

15. When is the *King* entitled to, and what are called, *royal fish?* 290.

16. What constitutes the *wreck* which belongs to the *King?* 290—292.

17. What are things *jetsam*, *flotsam*, and *ligan*, and to whom do they belong? 292, 293.

18. What is enacted, by statute 27 Edw. III. c. 13., if any ship be lost on the shore, and the goods come to land; what, by the *common law*, if any person but the *sheriff* take such goods; and what is enacted to assist ships in distress, by statutes 12 Ann. st. 2. c. 18. and 4 Geo. I. c. 12 ? 293.

19. What if any person secrete any of such goods ; and what is the offence of doing any act whereby the ship is lost or destroyed ? 293, 294.

20. What is enacted by the statute 26 Geo. II. c. 19. as to plundering any vessel in distress or wrecked, and to pilfering any goods cast ashore? 294.

21. What are *royal* mines, to which the *King* is entitled ? 294, 295.

22. What constitutes the *treasure-trove*, which belongs to the *King* ? 295.

23. What are *waifs*, and when do they belong to the *King*? 296, 297.

24. What are *estrays*, and what must be done in order to vest an absolute property in them in the *King* ? 297, 298.

25. What is one general reason why *royal fish*, *ship-wrecks*, *treasure-trove*, *waifs*, and *estrays*, should belong to the *King* ? 298, 299.

26. What are *bona confiscata,* or *forisfacta,* and why
    are they vested by law in the *King* ?   299.

27. What is a *deodand,* and for what purpose is it
    forfeited to the *King ?*   300—302.

28. Is the law of *deodands* different in the case of
    an *adult* and that of a *child,* and why is it
    so ?   300.

29. By whom is the *deodand* presented ?   301.

30. Are *wrecks, treasure-trove, royal fish, mines,
    waifs, estrays, deodands,* and *forfeitures,* now
    actually in the possession of the *King ?* 302.

31. When does an *escheat* of lands to the *King*
    happen ?   302.

32. What is an *idiot* or *natural fool;* and why has
    the *King* the custody of him and of his
    lands, as a branch of his *ordinary revenue ?*
    302—304.

33. By whom must the writ *de idiota inquirendo*
    be tried ; and in what event may the *King*
    grant the profits of his lands and the custody
    of his person ?   303.

34. What is a *lunatic* or *non compos mentis;* and
    how is it declared by the statute 17 Edw. II.
    c. 10. that the *King* shall have the guardian-
    ship of such an one ?   304.

35. What does the statute for regulating private
    mad-houses, 26 Geo. III. c. 91., enact ?   To
    be answered from Mr. Justice Christian's
    note (16) to this chapter.   304.

36. What is the method of proving a person *non compos*? 305.

37. Who is generally appointed *committee* of the lunatic's *person*, and who of his *estate*? 305.

38. What has chiefly occasioned the necessity of granting to the *King* his *extraordinary*, or second kind of, *revenue*? 306.

39. In what does this *revenue* consist, and by whom is it granted? 307.

40. Of what two natures are the *taxes*, which are raised upon the subject, to feed this *revenue*? 308.

41. What are the two usual *taxes* of the first nature? 308.

42. What were *tenths* and *fifteenths*? 308, 309.

43. What were *scutages*? 309, 310.

44. What were *hydages* and *talliages*? 310.

45. What were the *subsidies* which succeeded these last? 310—312.

46. How did *ecclesiastical subsidies* differ from *lay* ones; and what recompense was given to the *beneficed clergy*, when they were taxed equally with the *laity*? 311.

47. What is the present *land-tax*? 312, 313.

48. What is the *malt-tax*? 313.

49. What are the eight taxes of the second nature? 313. 318. 321. 323—326.

50. What are the *customs*, and what were said to be the two considerations upon which this *revenue* (or the more ancient part of it,

which arose only from *exports*) was invested in the *King*? 313—318.

51. How came *wool, skins*, and *leather* to be styled the *staple* commodities of the kingdom? 314.

52. Why cannot particularly the first of these articles be said, in its original sense, to be now the *staple* commodity of the kingdom? 314.

53. What was the hereditary *duty* belonging to the *crown*, called the *prisage* or *butlerage* of *wines*, and for what was it exchanged? 315.

54. What were *subsidies, tonnage*, and *poundage,* and what became of the last two *duties?* 315, 316.

55 What is called the *alien's duty?* 316.

56. What is the *excise duty*, and wherein does it differ from the *customs?* 318—320.

57. What is the *salt duty?* 321.

58. What is the *duty for the carriage of letters?* 321.

59. What are the *stamp duties?* 323.

60. What is the *duty upon houses and windows?* 324, 325.

61. What was *hearth-money?* 324.

62. What is the *duty for every male servant?* 325.

63. What is the *hackney-coach* and *chair duty?* 325.

64. What is the *duty on offices and pensions?* 326.

65. How is the *revenue* first and principally appropriated? 326.

66. What is the nature of the *national debt?* 326, 327.

67. Into what three principal *funds* are the produces of the several *taxes* consolidated? 329.

68. How are the surplusses of these *funds* disposed of? 330.

69. But for what purpose does the surplus of the *aggregate fund* first stand mortgaged by *parliament?* 331.

70. What is the amount of His present Majesty's *civil list?* 331.

71. What are the expenses defrayed by the *civil list?* 332.

72. Has the power of the *crown*, upon the whole, been weakened or strengthened by any transactions in the last century? 334—337.

CHAP. IX.

Of subordinate Magistrates.

1. WHAT are the six classes of *subordinate magistrates* of the most general use and authority? 339.

2. What is the *sheriff*, and by whom is he chosen? 339, 340.

3. In what one county does the office of *sheriff* still continue hereditary; and in what one instance is the inheritance of a *shrievalty* vested in a *corporate body* by *charter?* 340.

4. What are *pocket sheriffs?* 342.

5. What is the duration in office of a *sheriff;* how can his office be determined ; but what does the statute 1 Ann. st. 1. c. 8. enact, as to the duration in office of all officers appointed by the *King;* and what is enacted as to the man who has served the office of *sheriff,* by statute 1 Ric. II. c. 11. ? 342, 343.

6. What are the *sheriff's* four powers and duties ? 343.

7. What does he do, in his *judicial capacity?* 343.

8. What are his rank and duty, as *keeper of the King's peace?* 343.

9. What is he bound to do, in his *ministerial capacity?* 344.

10. What is his business, as the *King's bailiff?* 344.

11. What are the *sheriff's inferior officers?* 345.

12. What are the regulations of an *under-sheriff?* 345.

13. What two classes of *bailiffs* are there; and what are the duties of each class ? 345.

14. What is the business of *gaolers?* 346.

15. What is the *coroner;* how many *coroners* are there for each *county;* and by whom are they chosen ? 346.

16. What is the qualification for a *coroner;* and how has the office been abused ? 347, 348.

17. What is the *duration* of the office ? 348.

18. What are the *judicial* office and power of a *coroner?* 348.

19. What is the *ministerial* office of a *coroner?* 349.

20. What is the *custos rotulorum?* 349.
21. Who are *custodes* or *conservatores pacis, vii tute officii?* 349, 350.
22. What is the origin of the modern *justices of the peace?* 351.
23. How are they appointed? 351.
24. Who are called *justices of the quorum,* and why are they so called? 351.
25. What are the number and qualifications of these *justices?* 352, 353.
26. By what five causes is the office determinable? 353.
27. What are the power, office, and duty of a *justice of the peace?* 353, 354.
28. What two sorts of *constables* are there? 355,
29. By whom are they appointed? 355, 356.
30. What are the three principal duties of all *constables?* 356, 357.
31. By whom are *surveyors of the highways* constituted? 357.
32. To what four duties has the statute now reduced their office? 358.
33. What is the origin of *overseers of the poor?* 859.
34. By whom are they appointed, and what are their qualifications? 360.
35. What are their two principal offices and duties? 360.
36. What are the different ways in which such a *settlement* in a parish, as will entitle a per-

son to relief from the *overseers of the poor,*
may be gained ?   363.

37. In what case may a person be removed to
his own parish, and by whom ?   364.

38. What is the great cause of the inadequacy
of our *poor-laws.*   365.

———

CHAP. X.

Of the People, whether Aliens, Denizens, or Natives.

1. What is the first and most obvious division
of the *people* ?   366.

2. What is *allegiance* ?   366.

3. What was *fealty* ?   367.

4. What was the difference between *simple* and
liege homage ?   367.

5. For what reason, with us in England, could
only the *oath of fealty* be taken to *inferior
lords,* and not that of *allegiance* ?   367.

6. What is the present *oath of allegiance* ?   368.

7. What is the *oath of supremacy* ?   368.

8. What is the *oath of abjuration* ?   368.

9. By whom must this *oath* be taken; and to
whom may it be tendered ?   368.

10. To whom may the *oath of allegiance* be tendered ?   368.

11. Does the subject owe no *allegiance*, if he have taken no *oath*? 368, 369.

12. Into what two sorts or species, is all *allegiance*, both *express* and *implied*, distinguished by the *law*? 369.

13. What is the first of these kinds of *allegiance*? 369.

14. Can this *allegiance* be put off by any act of the *liegeman*? 369, 370.

15. What is the second of these kinds of *allegiance*; and when does it cease to be due? 370.

16. Is it *treason* for any subject to practise any thing against the *crown and dignity* of an usurper, who may be *King de facto?* 370, 371.

17. Is *allegiance* held to be applicable further than to the *political* capacity of the *King*? 371.

8. Do the different *rights* of *natives* and *aliens* correspond with their different degrees of *duty*? 371.

19. If an *alien* born purchase *lands* in England, who is entitled to them? 372.

20. Is the case altered, if the property he acquires be *personal estate*? 372.

21. May an *alien* trade or work for himself as an artificer in England? 372.

22. May an *alien* bring an action, or make a *will*? 372.

23. What if he be an *alien enemy*? 372.

24. In what cases is one born out of the *King's* dominions not an *alien*, but a *native*? 373.

CHAP. XI.

Of the Clergy.

7. What are the power and authority of an *archbishop*? 380.
8. What is called the *archbishop's options*? 381.
9. What are the privileges of the *Archbishop of Canterbury*? 381.
10. What are the power and authority of a *bishop*? 382.
11. How may *archbishopricks* and *bishopricks* become void? 382.
12. What are the offices of *dean* and *chapter*? 382.
13. How are ancient and modern *deans* elected? 382.
14. How is the *chapter* appointed? 383.
15. How may *deaneries* and *prebends* become void? 383.
16. What is the *jurisdiction* of an *archdeacon*; and by whom is he appointed? 383.
17. What are *rural deans*? 384.
18. What is a *parson*, and to what is he entitled? 384.
19. What is an *appropriated parsonage*; whence is the origin of *appropriations*; and whose consents are necessary to make an *appropriation*? 384, 385.
20. How may an *appropriation* be severed? 385, 386.
21. What is a *vicar*, and how is he distinguished from a *parson*? 388.
22. What four requisites are necessary to a *parson* or *vicar*; what is the qualification to be

6

admitted to a *benefice* by statute 13 & 14
Car. II. c. 4. ; and what if *orders*, or a licence
to preach be obtained by money or corrupt
practices ? 388, 389.

23. Upon what three accounts may the *bishop*
refuse to institute a *clerk* to a *parsonage* or
vicarage ? 389.

24. In the case of an *action* at *law*, brought by
the *patron* against the *bishop*, for refusing
his *clerk*, what if the cause be of a *temporal*
nature, what if of a *spiritual*, and what if it
be *minus sufficiens in literaturâ* ? 390.

25. What is required of a *vicar*, upon *institution* ?
390.

26. What is a *collation* to a *benefice* ? 391.

27. How is the ceremony of *induction* performed ?
391.

28. What is the *law* as to *residence*, by statute
21 Hen. VIII. c. 13. ; and what provision is
made for rebuilding or repairing *parsonage
houses*, by statute 17 Geo. III. c. 53 ? 392. ;
and see Mr. J. Christian's note (28) to this
chapter.

29. By what five means may a *parson* or *vicar*
cease to be so ? 392.

30. Who, by statute 21 Hen. VIII., are entitled
to have a dispensation, without which in
what case cannot two *benefices* be held together ? 392.

31. What are a *commenda retinere* and a *commenda recipere* ? 393.

———

CHAP. XII.

Of the Civil State.

11. How are *peers* now created, and what are the several advantages of both modes of creation? 400.

12. What are the privileges of *peers*, exclusive of their capacity as *members of parliament,* and as hereditary *counsellors of the crown?* 401, 402.

13. In what cases has a *peeress* a right to be tried by *peers?* 401.

14. How may a *peer* lose his *nobility?* 402.

15. Into what eleven degrees are the *commonalty* divided? 403—407.

16. By whom was the *order of the garter* instituted? 403.

17. What is a *knight banneret,* and in what case is he entitled to rank before the *younger sons of viscounts?* 403.

18. For what purpose was the title of *baronet* instituted; and for what reason have all *baronets* a *hand gules in a field argent* added to their *coat?* 403.

19. Why are *knights of the bath* so called? 404.

20. Whence is the origin of a *knight bachelor?* 404

21. Who are *esquires?* 406.

22. Who are *gentlemen?* 406.

23. Who are *yeomen?* 406.

24. What are the rest of the *commonalty?* 407.

CHAP. XIII.

Of the Military and Maritime States.

1. What does the *military state* include ?   408.
2. How do the laws and constitution of this kingdom look upon a *soldier ?*   408.
3. Of what does the *military state*, by the standing constitutional *law*, consist ?   412.
4. How is the *militia* of each county raised and officered ; and where are they not compellable to march ?   412.
5. How are the *armies*, which are esteemed necessary, when the nation is engaged in war, to be looked upon ?   413.
6. What is *martial law*, according to Sir Matthew Hale ?   413.
7. If a *lieutenant* or other, that hath commission of *martial authority*, doth, in time of peace, execute any man by colour of *martial law*, what is his crime by *magna carta ?*   413.
8. What does the *petition of right* moreover enact as to *soldiers* and *martial law ?*   413.
9. What does one of the articles of the *bill of rights* say as to *standing armies ?*   413.
10. In what case are *standing armies, ipso facto,* disbanded at the expiration of every year ?   414.
11. What does Baron Montesquieu declare to

be necessary to prevent the *executive power* from being able to oppress by its *armies?* 414.

12. How are our *armies* governed ?   414, 415.

13. What reform in the *mutiny act* does the commentator recommend ?   415, 416.

14. But in what cases has the humanity of our *standing laws* put *soldiers* in a better condition than other subjects ?   417.

15. Of what does the *maritime state* consist ?   418.

16. What are called the *laws of Oleron ?*   418.

17. How has the law, from necessity, provided for the supply of the *royal navy* with *seamen ?* 419.

18. How is it proved that the *King* has the power of *impressing sea-faring men* for the *sea-service ?*   419, 420.

19. Who are privileged from being *impressed* at common law ?   420.

20. How else has the *law* provided for the increase of *seamen* and manning the *royal navy ?*   420.

21. How is the *navy* governed; wherein does that method of government differ from that of the *army*; and whence is it most probable the difference arose ?   420, 421.

22. What are the privileges conferred on *sailors* 421.

CHAP. XIV.

Of Master and Servant.

1. WHAT are the three great *private œconomical relations of persons ?* 422.

2. What is the fourth *private œconomical relation,* consequent upon the failure of the third, by the death of one of the parties? 422.

3. Can *slavery* subsist in England ? 423, 424.

4. Can *slavery* subsist any where, consistently with reason and the principles of *natural law ;* and why are the three origins of the *right of slavery* assigned by Justinian, built upon false foundations ? 423.

5. What is the first sort of *servants* acknowledged by the laws of England ? 425.

6. If the hiring of such *servant* be general, for what period does the law construe it to be ? 425.

7. Who are compellable by two *justices* to go out to *service* in husbandry or certain specific trades, for the promotion of honest industry ? 425.

8. What are the second species of *servants* called 426.

9. Who are compellable by two *justices* to take the children of poor persons as *apprentices* ? 426.

10. What are the third species of *servants,* and for what term are they hired ? 426.

11. How are they regulated ?   427.

12. What is the fourth species of *servants*, being rather in a superior, or ministerial, capacity ?   427.

13. What does a person gain by *service for a year*, or *apprenticeship* under *indentures* ?   427.

14. What does a person gain by *serving seven years*, as *apprentice* to a trade ?   427.

15. Are *apprenticeships* requisite for every trade, and for trading every where ?   428.

16. Is an actual *apprenticeship* to a trade for *seven years* necessary to entitle a person to exercise that trade ?   428.

17. May a *master*, or *master's wife* correct his *apprentice* or his *servant* ?   428.

18. What if a *servant* assault his *master* or his *master's wife* ?   428.

19. What may a *master* do towards others on behalf of his *servant* ?   429.

20. What does the law call *maintenance* ?   429.

21. What may a *servant* do towards others, on behalf of his *master* ?   429, 430.

22. In what case is the *master* answerable for the act of the *servant* ?   429, 430.

CHAP. XV.

Of Husband and Wife.

1. WHAT is the second *private œconomical relation of persons?* 433.

2. In what light does the *law* consider *marriage?* 433.

3. When does the *law* allow the *marriage contract* to be good and valid? 433.

4. Of what two sorts are the disabilities to contract *marriage?* 434.

5. How do *canonical impediments* affect a *marriage?* 434.

6. What are the disabilities of this nature? 434.

7. What does the statute 32 Hen. VIII. c. 38. declare as to *marriages?* 435.

8. How do *civil disabilities* affect a *marriage?* 435.

9. What is the first of these *legal disabilities?* 436.

10. What is the second? 436.

11. What is the third? 437.

12. To what penalty is that *clergyman* liable, who marries a couple, either without publication of *banns*, or without a *licence?* 437.

13. To what penalty is he liable by statute 4 & 5 Ph. & M. c. 8. who marries a female under the age of sixteen years, without consent of her *parents* or *guardians?* 437.

14. What *marriages* without consent are void by statute 26 Geo. II. c. 33.? 437, 438.

15. What is the fourth legal incapacity to contract *marriage;* and what has the statute
15 Geo. II. c. 30. provided as to this incapacity? 438, 439.

16. How must a *marriage* be celebrated to make
it valid? 439, 440.

17. In what two ways may *marriages* be dissolved? 440.

18. What are the two kinds of *divorce?* 440.

19. For what cause must the first kind of *divorce*
be? 440.

20. For what causes must the second kind of
divorce be? 440, 441.

21. In case of *divorce à mensa et thoro,* what
does the law allow to the *wife?* 441.

22. What is the writ *de estoveriis habendis?* 441.

23. But in what case does the law allow no *ali-
mony?* 442.

24. What are the legal consequences of *marriage?* 442.

25. For what *debts* of the *wife* is the *husband*
liable? 442, 443.

26. Is there not one case where the *wife* shall
sue and be sued as a *feme sole?* 443.

27. Is there not one case where a *wife* by statute
3 Hen. VII. c. 2. can be evidence against
her *husband?* 443.

28. What is the only *deed* a *wife* can execute?
444.

29. What restraint may a *husband* lay upon his
wife, in case of gross misbehaviour? 444, 445.

CHAP. XVI.

Of Parent and Child.

1. WHAT is the third, and most universal *private œconomical relation of persons?* 446.
2. Of what two sorts are *children?* 446.
3. Who is a *legitimate child?* 446.
4. What are the three legal duties of *parents* to *legitimate children?* 446.
5. In what case may the *churchwardens* and *overseers* of the parish seize the *parent's* rents, goods and chattels, and dispose of them towards the *child's maintenance?* 448.
6. In what case shall a second *husband* be charged to maintain his *wife's child* by her first *husband?* 448.
7. But in what case is a *parent* not bound to provide a *maintenance* for his *issue?* 449.
8. What is the penalty on a *parent's* refusing to provide a *maintenance* for such of his *children* as the law puts upon him to maintain? 449.
9. What is enacted, if a *popish* or *Jewish parent* shall refuse to allow his *protestant child* a fitting *maintenance?* 449.
10. What is the law as to disinheriting *children* by *will?* 449, 450.
11. What may a *parent* do for a *child,* as its *protector,* towards others? 450.

12. In what one case does the law interfere between a *parent* and his *child*, in regard to
education?   451.

13. From what is the *power* of *parents* over their
children derived ?   452.

14. What power do our *laws* give a *parent* over
his *child?*   452, 453.

15. When does that power cease?   453.

16. Whence do the *duties* of *children* to their
parents arise ?   453.

17. What are those duties ?   453, 454.

18. Do these duties cease upon any misbehaviour
of the *parent ?*   454.

19. Who is a *bastard ?*   454.

20. Why is our law, on this head, superior to
the Roman ?   455.

21. What is a *writ de ventre inspiciendo ;* and by
whom and when may it be sued out?   456.

22. If a *man* dies and his *widow* marries again so
soon, that, by the course of nature, the *child*
of which she shall be delivered might have
been begotten by either *husband,* which shall
be the *child's father ?*   457.

23. In what cases may *children* born during *wed-
lock* be *bastards ?*   457.

24. What is the duty of *parents* to their *bastard
children ?*   458.

25. What is the method in which the English law
provides *maintenance* for *bastards?*   458.

26. What are the rights of a *bastard ?*   459.

27. What is the principal incapacity of a *bastard*? 459.

28. How may a *bastard* be made *legitimate*? 459.

CHAP. XVII.

Of Guardian and Ward.

1. WHAT is the fourth *private œconomical relation of persons*? 460.

2. What is the first species of *guardian*; and who is that *guardian*? 461.

2. If the *father* assign no *guardian* to his *daughter*, under the age of sixteen years, who shall be her *guardian*? 461.

4. What, and who is the second species of *guardian*? 461.

5. What is the third species of *guardian*; when does it take place; upon whom does that *guardianship* devolve till the *minor* is presumed to have sufficient discretion to choose his own guardian; and at what age does that presumption take place? 461, 462.

6. What is the fourth species of *guardian*; how may it be appointed; and who may accept the appointment? 462.

7. What are the power and reciprocal duty of a *guardian* and *ward*? 462.

8. What is the *guardian* bound to do when the *ward* comes of age ?   463.

9. Under whose control are *guardians* ? 463.

10. What are the different ages at which *male* and *female* are competent to different pur- poses ? 463.

11. On what day is the full *age* of *male* and *female* completed ?   463.

12. How can an *infant* be sued ?   464.

13. How can he sue ?   464.

14. At what age may an *infant* be *capitally punished* ? 464.

15. What, if an *infant* neglect to demand his right ?   465.

16. What estates may an *infant* aliene ?   465.

17. What legal act may an *infant* do ?   465.

18. How may an *infant* purchase lands ?   466.

19. What *deed* can an *infant* make which is not afterwards voidable ?   466.

20. How may an *infant* bind himself by *con- tract* ?   466.

CHAP. XVIII.

Of Corporations.

1. WHAT are *bodies politic, bodies corporate, or corporations ;* and for what purpose are they constituted ?   467.

2. What is the first division of *corporations ?* 469.

3. How are these *incorporations* again divided ? 470.

4. Of what two sorts are *lay corporations ?* 470.

5. What is absolutely necessary to the erection of a *corporation ?* 472.

6. In what sort of *corporations* is the *King's implied* consent to be found ? 472.

7. What are the two methods by which the *King's express* consent is given ? 473.

8. What is necessary to the very being of a *corporation ?* 475.

9. What are the five powers incident to all *corporations ?* 475, 476.

10. What are those privileges and disabilities that attend *aggregate corporations,* and are not applicable to such as are *sole ?* 476, 477.

11. May either kind of *corporation* take goods and chattels for the benefit of themselves and their successors ? 477.

12. Who have the right to give *laws* to *ecclesiastical* and *eleemosynary foundations ?* 477.

13. What acts can *aggregate corporations,* that have by their constitution a *head,* do, during the vacancy of the *headship ?* 478.

14. In *aggregate corporations,* what determines the act of the whole *body ;* and what is enacted by statute 33 Hen. VIII. c. 27., as to any private statutes made by *founders* of *corporations* in derogation of the *common law,* in this particular ? 478.

15. How do the statutes of *mortmain* affect *corporations?* 479.

16. What is the general duty of *corporations?* 480.

17. How is this duty enforced? 480.

18. Who is the visitor of *ecclesiastical corporations?* 480.

19. Who is the visitor of *lay corporations?* 480.

20. What does the law mean by the distinction of *fundatio incipiens,* and *fundatio perficiens;* and why is the King the visitor of all *lay civil corporations,* and the *endower* the visitor of all *lay eleemosynary* ones? 481.

21. Where shall the *King* exercise this his jurisdiction? 481.

22. May there not be another visitor of *lay eleemosynary corporations* than the *founder?* 482.

23. What has been long held as to the *visitation* of *hospitals, spiritual* and *lay;* what does the statute 14 Eliz. c. 5. direct on the subject; and by whom are all the *hospitals* founded by the statute 39 Eliz. c.5. to be visited? 482.

24. Are *colleges lay* or *ecclesiastical corporations?* 483.

25. To whom do the lands and tenements of a *corporation* revert, upon its dissolution? 484.

26. What becomes of the *corporation's* debts, upon its dissolution? 484.

27. By what four methods may a *corporation* be dissolved? 485.

28. What is an *information in nature of a writ of quo warranto*; and when may it be brought? 485.
29. What is enacted as to the *franchises* of the *city of London*? 485.
30. What is provided against the dissolution of *corporations*? 485.

THE END OF THE FIRST BOOK.

BOOK THE SECOND.

OF THE RIGHTS OF THINGS.

—

CHAPTER I.

Of Property in general.

1. WHAT do the writers on natural law style those rights which a man may acquire in and to such external things as are unconnected with his person ?   1.
2. In what has all dominion over external things its original ?   2.
3. In those times when all things were in common among men, what first gave to one man a transient property in the *use* of a thing ?   3.
4. What circumstances must soon have pointed out the necessity of appropriating to individuals not the immediate *use* only, but the *substance* of the thing to be used ; and how must that property have been originally acquired ?   4—9.
5. What was the origin of *conveyances, wills, heirships,* and *escheats* ?   9—13.

22. Why could not a bastard be born a *villein*? 94.

23. In what cases had the *villein* remedy at law against the *lord*?   94.

24. How might a *villein* be enfranchised ?   94.

25. What was *implied manumission* ?   94, 95.

26. How came *villeins* to be called *tenants by copy of court-roll*?   95.

27. How did *villenage* decline and fall ?   95, 96.

28. From what has been premised, what two indispensable principles of copyhold tenure may we collect ?   97.

29. In what degree have the customs of *manors* superseded the will of the *lord* ?   97.

30. What four fruits and appendages has a *copyhold tenure*, whether of inheritance or for life, in common with *free tenures* ?   97.

31. What three besides has a *copyhold* ?   97.

32. What is a *heriot* ?   97.

33. What is *wardship* in *copyhold estates* ?   98.

34. What are *fines*; and what has the law declared to be the *ultimatum* of their amount ?   98.

35. What was *privileged villenage*, or *villein socage* ?   99.

36. What species of our modern *tenures* has arisen from this antient one ?   99.

37. Of what does *antient demesne* consist ?   99.

38. What immunities have *tenures* of *antient demesne*; and in what do lands holden by this *tenure* differ from common *copyholds* ?   99—101.

8. Does either of these .kinds of *things real* include the other? 17.
9. Of what two kinds are *hereditaments;* and of
what do each of those kinds consist? 17.
10. Under what general denomination may all
corporeal hereditaments be comprehended?
17.
11 If I convey the *land,* doth the *structure* upon
it pass with it? 18.
12. How is *water* considered in law; and by
what description must an *action* be brought
to recover it? 18.
13. What extent hath *land,* it its legal signification, upwards and downwards? 18.
14. What passes in law, by a grant of *water?* 19

———

CHAP. III.

Of Incorporeal Hereditaments.

1. WHAT is an *incorporeal hereditament?* 20
2. Of what ten sorts do *incorporeal hereditaments*
principally consist? 21.
3. What is an *advowson?* 21.
4. What is the difference between an *advowson
appendant* and an *advowson in gross?* 22.
5. What is an advowson *presentative?* 22.
6. What is an advowson *collative?* 22.
7. What is an advowson *donative?* 23.

8. What are *tithes*, whether *predial, mixed*, or *personal?*   24.

9. To whom are they due?   28.

10. By what two means may lands be discharged from the payment of *tithes?*   28.

11. What is a *real composition;* and by what means has it grown into desuetude?   28, 29.

12. What is a *modus decimandi,* or *modus* only, as it is called?   29.

13. What six rules must be observed to make the *modus* good and sufficient?   30.

14. What is a *rank modus?*   30.

15. What is a prescription *de non decimendo?*   31.

16. Who are personally entitled to the privilege of being discharged from the payment of *tithes?*   31.

17. From what original have sprung all the lands, which, being in *lay* hands, do at present claim to be *tithe free?*   32.

18. What is right of *common?*   32.

19. Of what four sorts does *common* chiefly consist?   32.

20. What is *common of pasture;* and of what four species does it consist?   32.

21. What is common *appendant?*   33.

22. What is common *appurtenant?*   33.

23. What is common *because of vicinage?*   33.

24. What is common *in gross?*   34.

25. What is called a lord of a manor's *approving?*   34.

26. What is common of *piscary?*   34.
27. What is common of *turbary?*   34.
28. What is common of *estrovers*, or *botes?*   35.
29. What is *right of way;* and on what three reasons may it be grounded?   35, 36.
30. Upon what principle of law, when a man grants me a piece of ground in the middle of his field, does he, at the same time, tacitly and impliedly give me a *way* to come at it?   36.
31. What are *offices?*   36.
32. What are *dignities?*   37.
33. What are *franchises* or *liberties?*   37.
34. Wherein do a *forest*, a *chace*, and a *park* differ?   38.
35. What is a *free-warren?*   38, 39.
36. How comes it to pass that a man and his heirs have sometimes *free-warren* over another's ground?   39.
37. What is a *free-fishery;* and by what was the making *grants* of such a franchise prohibited?   39.
38. Wherein does a *free-fishery* differ from a *several* one, and a *common of piscary?*   39, 40.
39. What are *corodies?*   40.
40. What is an *annuity;* and wherein does it differ from a *rent-charge?*   40.
41. What are *rents?*   41.
42. What are the four requisites to a *rent?*   41.
43. What are the three manner of *rents*, at common law?   41.

CHAP. IV.

Of the Feodal System.

6. Upon the introduction of the *feodal* system into England, what became the fundamental maxim and necessary principle of our English tenures ?   51.

7. How was the *feodal* system affected by King Henry I.'s charter ?   52.

8. How by that of King John, confirmed by his son Henry III. ?   52.

9. What were the grantor and grantee of a *feud* respectively called ?   53.

10. What was the ceremony of granting a *feud ?*   53.

11. What were the oaths of *fealty* and *homage* ?   53, 54.

12. What was the two-fold nature of the feudatory's *service* or *suit ?*   54.

13. Why were the feudatories distinguished by the appellation of *pares curtis* or *curiæ ?*   54.

14. How were *feuds* hereditary ?   55, 56.

15. Why could neither the *lord* nor the *vassal* aliene their estates without the consent of each other ?   57.

16. Whence came *feodal* tenures to be divided into *feoda propria et impropria ;* and what was the difference between such *feuds ?*   57, 58.

CHAP. V.

Of the antient English Tenures.

1. WHY are the words *tenement*, *tenant*, and *tenure*, so universally applied in speaking of all the real property of the kingdom ? 59.

2. Who is the lord *paramount* of England ? 59.

3. Who were called *tenants paravail* ? 60.

4. Who were called *tenants in capite* ? 60.

5. Of what two kinds, in respect of their quality, were the *services* that were due on account of the four principal species of *lay tenure*, to which all other *tenures*, that subsisted among our ancestors, may be reduced ? 60.

6. Of what two kinds were they, in respect of their quantity, and the time of exacting them ? 60.

7. What were *free* services ? 60.

8. What were *base* services ? 61.

9. What were the *certain* services ? 61.

10. What were the *uncertain* services ? 61.

11. What, according to Bracton, were these four principal species of *lay-tenure*, to which all other *tenures*, that subsisted among our ancestors, may be reduced ? 61, 62.

12. What constituted a *tenure* by *knight-service*, and what was the *service* ? 62.

13. What was this tenant's *reditus*, his *rent* or *service*, for the land he claimed to hold ? 62.

9

14. What were the seven fruits and consequences inseparably incident to this *tenure ?* 63.

15. What were the three principal *aids* which were taken by the *lord* of this *tenant ?* 63.

16. What did King John's *magna carta* ordain as to *aids ?* 64.

17. What did the statute, called *confirmatio chartarum*, ordain as to *aids ?* 64.

18. What did the *statute of Westminster* fix as to *aids ?* 65.

19. What was *relief*, and how was it compounded for ? 65, 66.

20. What was *primer seisin ?* 66.

21. What was *wardship ?* 67.

22. What was *livery* or *ousterlemain ?* 68.

23. What was an *inquisitio post mortem ?* 68.

24. Who was compelled to receive the *order of knighthood*, or to pay a *fine* to the *King ?* 69.

25. What was the right of *marriage (maritagium*, as contradistinguished from *matrimonium) ?* 70.

26. What were *fines upon alienation ?* **71.**

27. What was an *attornment ?* 72.

28. What was *escheat ?* 72.

29. What was the *tenure* by *grand serjeanty, per magnum servitium !* 73.

30. What was *tenure* by *cornage ?* 74.

31. What was *tenure* by *scutage*, or *escuage, servitium scuti ?* 74.

32. What did *magna carta* declare as to *scutage ?* 74.

33. By what means were all the advantages of the feodal constitution destroyed ? 75.
34. To whom do we owe the plan for the abolition of the feodal system ? 76, 77.
35. What actually gave it its death-blow ? 77.

CHAP. VI.

Of the modern English Tenures.

1. WHAT, in its most general and extensive signification, is *socage*, to which all *tenures* except *frankalmoign, grand serjeanty,* and *copyhold* were reduced, upon the abolition of the feodal system ? 78, 79.
2. Of what two sorts is *socage* ? 79.
3. What is the etymology of the word ? 80, 81.
4. Does *free* and *common socage tenure* remain in any part of England to this day ; and what people's liberty does that remnant prove *socage* to have been ? 81.
5. Since the certainty of its *services* is the grand criterion of *socage*, what will this species of *tenure* include ? 81.
6. What is *petit-serjeanty* ? 82.
7. What is *tenure in burgage* ? 82.
8. What is the custom of *borough English* ? 83.

9. What are the four distinguishing properties of *tenure* in *gavelkind*?   84.

10. In what points does *tenure* in *free socage* partake of the feodal nature?   85—89.

11. But wherein did the *socage* and the *feodal tenures* widely differ as to *service, relief, wardship*, and *marriage*?   86—89.

12. When was the *feodal tenure* abolished and sunk into the *socage*?   89.

13. What species of our modern *tenures* has arisen from *pure villenage*?   90.

14. What is a *manor*?   90.

15. What was the difference between *book-land* and *folk-land*?   90.

16. What is a *court-baron*; and what happens if the number of suitors should not be sufficient to make a *jury of two*?   90, 91.

17. What is an *honour*?   91.

18. What did the 32d chapter of *magna carta*, 9 Hen. III., and the *statute of Wesminster* declare as to all sales or feoffments of land; and what is now therefore essential to a *manor*?   91, 92.

19. What were *pure villeins*; and of what two classes?   92—94.

20. What was a *neife*?   94.

21. In case of a marriage between a *freeman* and a *neife*, or a *villein* and a *freewoman*, were the issue *free* or *villein*?   94.

22. Why could not a bastard be born a *villein?* 94.

23. In what cases had the *villein* remedy at law against the *lord?* 94.

24. How might a *villein* be enfranchised? 94.

25. What was *implied manumission?* 94, 95.

26. How came *villeins* to be called *tenants by copy of court-roll?* 95.

27. How did *villenage* decline and fall? 95, 96.

28. From what has been premised, what two indispensable principles of copyhold tenure may we collect? 97.

29. In what degree have the customs of *manors* superseded the will of the *lord?* 97.

30. What four fruits and appendages has a *copyhold tenure*, whether of inheritance or for life, in common with *free tenures?* 97.

31. What three besides has a *copyhold?* 97.

32. What is a *heriot?* 97.

33. What is *wardship* in *copyhold estates?* 98.

34. What are *fines;* and what has the law declared to be the *ultimatum* of their amount? 98.

35. What was *privileged villenage*, or *villein socage?* 99.

36. What species of our modern *tenures* has arisen from this antient one? 99.

37. Of what does *antient demesne* consist? 99.

38. What immunities have *tenures* of *antient demesne;* and in what do lands holden by this *tenure* differ from common *copyholds?* 99—101.

CHAP. VII.

Of Freehold Estates of Inheritance.

6. Into what two species are *estates* of *freehold* of the former nature again divided ? 104.

7. Who is *tenant* in *fee simple*, or *tenant* in *fee?* 104.

8. What, and in contradistinction to what, is the true meaning of the word *fee* ? 104, 105.

9. By what words do we, in the most solemn acts of law, express the highest *estate* that any subject can have ? 105.

10. In contradistinction to what, has the word *fee* the adjunct of *simple* annexed to it ? 106.

11. Of what species of hereditaments can a man not be said to be seized, IN HIS DEMESNE, *as of fee?* 106, 107.

12. What word is necessary in the *grant* or *donation*, in order to make a *fee*, or *inheritance* ? 107, 108.

13. But by what five exceptions is this rule now softened ? 108, 109.

14. Into what two sorts may we divide limited *fees* ? 109.

15. What is a *base* or *qualified fee?* 109.

16. What was a *conditional fee* at the common law ? 110.

17. What did our ancestors hold with regard to the *condition* annexed to such a *fee?* 110, 111.

18. But what if the *tenant* did not in fact aliene the land, and if then both the *tenant* and the *issue* died ? 111.

19. What did the *statute of Westminster the second* (commonly called the statute *de-donis conditionalibus*) enact as to *conditional fees* ? 112.

20. Whence is the origin of *fee-tail* and *reversion?* 112.

21. What things may, and what may not, be *entailed* under the statute *de donis?* 113.

22. What is the first division of the several species of *estates tail?* 113.

23. What is *tail general?* 113.

24. What is *tail special?* 113, 114.

25. By what distinction are *estates* in *general* and *special tail* farther diversified? 114.

26. What word is necessary to make a *fee-tail?* 114, 115.

27. Is there not another species of *entailed estates*, now grown out of use, but still capable of subsisting in law? 115.

28. What is this defined to be? 115.

29. What are the four *incidents* to a *tenancy in tail* under the *statute of Westminster the second?* 115, 116.

30. What, and when, was declared the first sufficient *bar* of an *estate tail?* 116, 117.

31. Can an *estate tail* be forfeited to the King, upon any conviction of high treason? 117, 118.

32. Do *leases*, made by *tenants* in *tail*, bind the *issue* in *tail?* 118.

33. What construction was put upon the statute of *fines* by the statute 32 Hen. VIII. c. 36.? 118.

34. What exceptions were made by this statute as to *fines*, and by the statute 34 & 35 Hen. VIII. c. 20., as to *common recoveries?* 118, 119.

35. Of what debts are *estates tail* liable to the payment? 119.
36. What appointment of lands *entailed*, by tenant in *tail*, is good without *fine* or *recovery*? 119.
37. What difference is there, then, between the present *estates tail*, and the old *conditional fees* after the *condition* was performed? 119

———

CHAP. VIII.

Of Freeholds not of Inheritance.

1. OF what two species are such *estates* of *freehold* as are not of *inheritance*, but *for life* only? 120.
2. In what two ways may an *estate* of the first species be created? 120, 121.
3. What is a tenant *pur auter vie?* 120.
4. Against whom (with what exception) does the law say, that all grants are to be taken most strongly? 121.
5. Are there not some *estates* for *life*, which may determine before the *life* expires? 121.
6. Why, in *conveyances*, is the grant usually made " for the term of a man's *natural* life?" 121.
7. What are the two principal *incidents* to all *estates for life?* 122.
8. What are *emblements?* 122.

10

land, in order to entitle the *widow* to *dower?* 132.

25. What is usually called the *widow's free-bench?* 132.

26. What are the four species of *dower* now subsisting ? 132, 133.

27. Of what part of his lands, might a *husband* endow his *wife, ad ostium ecclesiæ ?* 133—135.

28. What is now the only usual species of *endowment ?* 135.

29. What is called the *widow's quarantine ?* 135.

30. What is a *writ of admeasurement of dower ?* 136.

31. How may *dower* be *barred* or prevented ? 136, 137.

32. How is a *jointure* defined by Sir Edward Coke ? 137.

33. What did the statute of *uses* provide as to *barring* a *wife* of *dower ?* 137, 138.

34. What four requisites must be punctually observed, to make a *jointure* good ? 138.

35. What if the *jointure* be made to the *wife after* marriage ? 138.

36. What if the *jointress* be evicted of her *jointure,* on account of its being made on a bad title ? 138.

37. What are the comparative advantages of situation, between *tenants in dower,* and *jointresses ?* 138, 139.

CHAP. IX.

Of Estates less than Freehold.

1. WHAT are the three sorts of *estates less than freehold?*   140.
2. What is an *estate for years?*   140.
3. What is a *month* in law?   141.
4. What is a lease for a *twelvemonth?*   141.
5. How many hours does the law reckon in the space of a day?   141.
6. How might a *lessee estate* be defeated by the antient law?   142.
7. What is an indispensable requisite to an *estate for years?*   143.
8. Why cannot a *lease for life* commence *in futuro,* though a *lease for years* may?   143, 144.
9. What right has a *tenant for years* in the *tenement?*   144.
10. Of what is he possessed, when he has entered the *tenement?*   144.
11. What is the legal difference between the *term* and the *time* of a *lease for years?*   144.
12. What are the *incidents* to an *estate for years?*   144, 145.
13. What is the difference of situation between a *tenant for life,* and a *tenant for years,* with regard to *emblements?*   145.
14. What is an *estate at will?*   145.

15. In what case is a *tenant at will* entitled to *emblements?* 146.

16. What act amounts to a determination of the *will* on either side ? 146.

17. How have courts of law leaned, in construing demises, where no certain *term* is mentioned ? 147.

18. What *notice* is requisite to determine a *tenancy from year to year?* 147.

19. In what one species of *estate at will*, is the *will* qualified by what ? 147, 148.

20. What seems to have been the reason why the *absolute freehold* was never granted by *lords* to their *villeins?* 148, 149.

21. What kind of *freehold* have *customary freeholders?* 149.

22. What are the comparative advantages of interest, between a *copyholder of inheritance, with a fine certain,* and an *absolute freeholder?* 150.

23. What is an *estate at sufferance ?* 150.

24. Against whom can no man be *tenant at sufferance ?* 150.

25. How must an owner of lands vary his proceeding in an *action of trespass* against a *tenant by sufferance,* from the same *action* against a stranger ? 150.

26. What have the statutes of 4 & 11 Geo. II. c. 28. and 19 enacted in the cases of a *tenant's holding over his term,* or his own *notice to quit ?* 151.

CHAP. X.

Of Estates upon Condition.

1. WHAT are *estates upon condition ?*   152.
2. Of what two sorts are *estates upon condition ?* 152.
3. What three other *conditional estates* are included under this last sort ?   152.
4. What are *estates upon condition implied in law* ?   152.
5. By what two breaches of an *implied condition* may an *office* be *forfeited?*   153.
6. How do a *public* and a *private office* differ in respect of *forfeit?*   153.
7. Upon what principle proceed all the *forfeitures,* which are given by law, of *life-estates* and others ?   153.
8. What is an *estate on condition expressed ?* 154.
9. Of what two sorts are *condition expressed?* 154.
10. What is an *estate* " to a man and his heirs, *tenants of the manor of Dale ?*"   154.
11. What is the distinction between a *condition in deed,* and a *limitation,* or *condition in law?* 155.
12. In all instances of *limitations* or *conditions subsequent,* where the *condition* is *contingent* and *uncertain,* what estate has the *grantee,* so long as the *condition* remain unbroken ?   156.
13. When are *conditions* void ?   156.

CHAP. XI.

Of Estates in Possession, Remainder and Reversion.

3. What is the difference between *estates executed* and *estates executory?*   163.
4. What.may an *estate in remainder* be defined to be ?   164.
5. When lands are granted to A. for twenty years, with *remainder* to B. and his heirs for ever, are not these two *estates ?* 164.
6. What are the three rules laid down by law to be observed in the creation of *remainders?* 165. 167, 168.
7. What is called the *particular estate ?*   165.
8. Why cannot an *estate* of *freehold* be created to commence *in futuro ?*   166.
9. Is a *remainder* an *estate* commencing *in præsenti* or *in futuro ?*   165, 166.
10. What *particular estate* will, and when will a *particular estate* not, *support* a *remainder over ?*   166, 167.
11. Can a *remainder* be granted of a *chattel-interest?*   167.
12. In what case is it necessary that a *lessee for years* should have *livery of seisin ?*   167.
13. Need the *precedent particular estate*, and the *remainder* be *in esse*, at one and the same time, *during the continuance of the first estate;* or what latitude is allowed ?   168.
14. Of what two sorts are *remainders ?* 168.
15. What are *vested* or *executed remainders?* 168, 169.
16. On account of what two sorts of uncertainty

may *remainders* be *contingent*, or *executory?* 169.

17. What is enacted by statute 10 & 11 W. III. c. 16 as to *posthumous children taking remainders?* 169.

18. What are *potentia propinqua*, and *potentia remotissima?* 170.

19. Why cannot a *contingent remainder* of *freehold* be limited on any *particular estate*, less than a *freehold?* 171.

20. How may *contingent remainders* be *defeated?* 171.

21. Is there no way of preventing this *defeat?* 171.

22. What is an *executory devise?* 172.

23. In what three points does it differ from a *remainder?* 172, 173.

24. Why may a *devise of freehold* commence *in futuro?* 173.

25. Within what time does the law's *abhorrence of a perpetuity* declare that the *contingencies* of an *executory devise* ought to be such as may happen? 173, 174.

26. Why does the law *abhor a perpetuity?* 174.

27. What has been settled in order, to prevent the danger of *perpetuities*, as to the persons to whom *remainders* may, by an *executory devise*, be limited over, after a *term* of years has been given to one man for his life; and what has been also settled, as to the *contin-*

CHAP. XII.

Of Estates in severalty, joint-tenancy, copar-cenary, and common.

6. Of what four kinds is the *unity* of a *joint-estate*? 180—182.

7. If an estate in fee be given to a man and his wife, how are they *seised*? 182.

8. Upon the decease of one *joint-tenant*, what share of the *estate* remains to the *survivor*; and why? 183, 184.

9 Why cannot the *King*, or any *corporation*, be *joint-tenant* with a private person? 184.

10. How may an estate in *joint-tenancy* be severed and destroyed? 185.

11. But why is a devise of one *joint-tenant*'s share by will, no *severance* of the *jointure*? 186.

12. In what case is it disadvantageous for *joint-tenants* to dissolve the *jointure*? 187.

13. What is an *estate* held in *coparcenary*? 187.

14. Who are *parceners* by common law? 187.

15. Who are *parceners* by particular custom? 187.

16. What are the properties of *parceners*? 188.

17. Which of the four *unities* of a *joint-estate* have *parceners*? 188.

18. In what five points do *parceners* differ from *joint-tenants*? 188.

19. What are the five methods in which *parceners* may make *partition*? 189.

20. What is the law of *hotchpot*, which is incident to this estate? 190, 191.

21. In what three ways may an *estate in coparcenary* be dissolved? 191.

22. Who are *tenants in common*? 191—193.

23. Which of the four *unities* of a *joint-estate* have *tenants in common ?*   191.

24. By what two means may *tenancy in common* be created ?   192, 193.

25. Does the law, in its construction of a *deed,* favour *joint-tenancy,* or *tenancy in common ?* 193.

26. What are the *incidents* attending a *tenancy in common ?*   194.

27. In what two ways only can *estates in common* be dissolved ?   194.

———

CHAP. XIII.

Of the Title to Things real, in general.

1. WHAT is the *title* to *things real ?*   195.

2. What are the four several stages or degrees, requisite to form a complete *title* to lands and tenements ? 195—197. 199.

3. What is the mere *naked possession ;* how may it happen; and in what degree is it a legal *title ?*   195, 196.

4. What are the two sorts of *right of possession ;* and by what means may the first grow into the second ?   196, 197.

5. What is the mere *right of property ;* and how can it recover the *right of possession ?*   197, 198.

CHAP. XIV.

Of Title by Descent.

1. By what two methods may the *title* to *things real* be reciprocally acquired on the one hand, and lost on the other? 201.
2. What is the *title* by *descent?* 201.
3. What is *consanguinity*; and of what two kinds? 202.
4. Wherein do these two kinds of *consanguinity* differ? 203, 204.
5. In what does the very being of *collateral consanguinity* consist? 205.
6. What is the method of computing the *degrees* of *collateral consanguinity?* 206, 207.
7. What is the first *rule*, or *canon*, of *inheritance*, according to which *estates* are transmitted from the ancestor to the heir? 208. 210.
8. What is the difference between an *heir apparent* and an *heir presumptive?* 208.
9. Who cannot be accounted such an ancestor, as that an *inheritance* of lands or tenements can be derived from him? 209.
10. What is the second *rule*, or *canon*, of *inheritance?* 212, 213.
11. What is the third *rule*, or *canon*, of *inheritance?* 214. 216.
12. What are exceptions to this rule? 216.

13. In what one *inheritance* does *succession* by *primogeniture* take place among females? 216.

14. In what one *inheritance* does *sole succession* take place among females? 216.

15. What is the fourth *rule*, or *canon*, of *inheritance*? 217.

16. When is an *inheritance* divided *per stirpes*, and when *per capita*? 217, 218.

17. What is the fifth *rule* or *canon*, of *inheritance*? 220. 222.

18. What is the great and general principle upon which the law of *collateral inheritances* depends? 223.

19. What is the sixth *rule*, or *canon*, of *inheritance*, being, like the seventh and last, only a *rule of evidence* who the *purchasing* ancestor was? 224.

20. Who is a *kinsman of the whole blood*? 227.

21. Why is the exclusion of a *kinsman of the half-blood* not unreasonable? 228—232.

22. What one *inheritance* may descend to the *half-blood* of the person last seised, so that it be the *blood* of the first *purchaser*; and why? 233.

23. For this reason, in what kind of *estate* is *half-blood* no impediment to the descent? 233.

24. What is the seventh and last *rule*, or *canon*, of *inheritance*? 234.

25. What is the most probable original of this *rule*? 235.

26. When is this *rule* totally reversed? 236.

CHAP. XV.

Of Title by Purchase, and first by Escheat.

1. WHAT is *purchase,* taken in its largest and most extensive sense ?   241.

2. If an *estate* be made to A. for life, *remainder* to his right heirs in *fee,* by what shall the heirs take ?   242.

3. What was meant by calling William the Norman *Conqueror ?*   243.

4. In what two points does the difference in effect, between the acquisition of an *estate* by *descent* and by *purchase,* principally consist ? 243, 244.

5. What five methods of acquiring a *title* to *estates* does *purchase* include ?   244.

6. What is *escheat ?*   244, 245.

7. Upon what principle is the law of *escheats* founded ?   245.

8. What are the first three cases wherein *inheritable blood* is wanting ?   246.

9. What is the fourth case, wherein *inheritable blood* is wanting ?   246, 247.

10. What is the fifth case ?   247, 248.

11. Who are *bastard eignè* and *mulier puisnè ;* and in what case may the former *bar* the latter of his *inheritance ;* and this for what three reasons ?   248.

12. What legal *heirs* can a *bastard* have ?   249.

13. What is the sixth case, wherein *inheritable blood* is wanting ?   249.

14. What is the difference of *inheritable* operation on the *blood* of *alien*, in the acts of *denization* and of *naturalization?*   249, 250.

15. If an *alien* come into England, and there have issue two sons, who are thereby *natural-born subjects*, and one of them purchase land and die, who cannot be his *heir;* and why?   250.

16. What is enacted by the statute 11 and 12 Will. III. c. 6., as to the *inheritance* of *natural-born subjects*, deriving their pedigrees through *aliens;* and how is this statute qualified by that of 25 Geo. II. c. 39.?   251.

17. What is the seventh case, wherein *inheritable blood* is wanting?   251.

18. What is the difference between *forfeitures* of *lands* to the *King*, and *escheat* to the *lord?* 251—254.

19. By what means only can the *corruption of blood* be absolutely removed?   254.

20. If a man *attainted* be pardoned by the King, can his son inherit?   254.

21. If a man have issue a son, and be *attainted*, and afterwards pardoned, and then have issue a second son and die, who cannot be his *heir;* and why?   255.

22. If the ancestor be *attained*, may his sons be *heirs* to each other?   255.

23. What is declared in most of the new *felonies*, created by act of parliament since the reign of Henry VIII.; and wherefore is it so? 256.

CHAP. XVI.

Of Title by Occupancy.

CHAP. XVII.

Of Title by Prescription.

1. WHAT is title by *prescription;* and how is it distinguished from *custom?* 263.
2. What is called *prescribing in a que estate?* 264.
3. What has the *statute of limitations,* 32 Hen. VIII. c. 2. enacted, as to *prescriptions?* 264.
4. What sort of *hereditaments* may be claimed by *prescription?* 264.
5. Why cannot a *prescription* give a *title* to lands? 264.
6. In whom must a *prescription* be laid? 265.
7. If the thing prescribed has what incapacity, why cannot the *prescription* be made? 265.
8. Why cannot *deodands, felons' goods,* and the like, be prescribed for, while *treasure-trove, waifs, estrays,* and the like, can? 265.
9. For what more may a man prescribe, *in himself and his ancestors,* than he may *in a que estate;* and why may he do so? 266.
10. Is there not a difference in the *inheritance* of a thing prescribed *in one's self, and one's ancestors,* and one prescribed *in a que estate?* 266.

CHAP. X.V*III*.

Of Title by Forfeiture.

1. WHAT is *forfeiture?* 267.
2. By what eight means, may lands, tenements, and hereditaments be *forfeited?* 267.
3. What are the six offences, which induce a *forfeiture* of lands and tenements to the crown? 267, 268.
4. Of what three kinds is the *alienation* contrary to law, which induces a *forfeiture?* 268.
5. What is *alienation* in *mortmain, in mortua manu?* 268.
6. How were *common recoveries* invented? 271.
7. How were *uses* and *trusts* invented? 272.
8. What is *licence of mortmain;* and how has it been dispensed with? 272, 273.
9. What is enacted by the statute 9 Geo. II. c. 36. as to lands and tenements, or money to be laid out thereon, given for or charged with, *charitable uses?* 273, 274.
10. Who are excepted out of this act; and with what proviso is the exception made? 274.
11. Why is *alienation* to an *alien,* a cause of forfeiture? 274.
12. When are *alienations* by *particular tenants forfeitures;* and to whom, and for what two reasons? 274, 275.

13. What is it, if *tenant in tail* alienes in *fee*; and why ?   275.

14. In case of *forfeiture* by *particular tenants*, what becomes of all legal *estates* by them before created ?   275.

15. What is *disclaimer*, in its nature and consequences ?   275, 276.

16. What is *forfeiture* by *lapse* ?   276.

17. In what two cases, can no right of *lapse* accrue ?   276.

18. What is the *term*, in which the *title* to present by *lapse* accrues ?   276, 277.

19. What if the *bishop* be both *patron* and *ordinary* ?   277.

20. What if the *bishop* or *metropolitan* do not *present* immediately upon *lapse* ?   277.

21. What if the *King* do not ?   277.

22. In what cases only, is the *bishop* required to give notice of a vacancy to the *patron*, in order to entitle him, the *metropolitan* and the *King* to the advantage of a *lapse* ?   278.

23. When does the law style the *bishop a disturber* ; and of what does it consequently deprive him ?   278.

24. What if the right of *presentation* be contested ?   278

25. What is *forfeiture* by *simony* ?   278, 279.

26. Is it *simony* to purchase a *presentation*, the *living* being actually vacant ?   279.

27. Is it *simony*, for a *clerk* to purchase the next presentation, and be thereupon presented? 279, 280.

28. Is it *simony*, for a *father* to purchase such a presentation for his *son ?* 280.

29. What, if a *simoniacal* contract be made with the *patron*, the *clerk* not being privy thereto *?* 280.

30. Are bounds given to pay money to charitable uses, on receiving a presentation to a *living*, *simoniacal?* 280.

31. What *bonds of resignation* are not *simoniacal?* 280.

32. Are general *bonds of resignation* legal? 280.

33. What are the only causes, for which the law will justify the patron's making use of such a general *bond of resignation?* 280.

34. Of what two kinds, are the *conditions*, the *breach* or *nonperformance* of which induces a *forfeiture?* 281.

35. What is *waste ;* and of what two kinds? 281.

36. What are the general heads of *waste* in *houses*, in *timber*, and in *land?* 281, 282.

37. Who are liable to be punished for *waste ;* and who not? 282, 283.

38. What is the punishment for committing *waste?* 283, 284.

39. By what may *copyhold estates* be *forfeited?* 284.

40. Who is a *bankrupt?* 285.

41. What becomes of a *bankrupt's* lands and tenements ? 285, 286.
42. With only what exception, has the statute 21 Jac. I. c. 19. authorised the disposal of a *bankrupt's estate tail* in *possession, remainder,* or *reversion ?* 286.

———

CHAP. XIX.

Of Title by Alienation.

1. WHAT is *alienation, conveyance,* or *purchase,* in its limited sense ? 287.
2. Who are capable of *conveying* and *purchasing ?* 290.
3. How alone may *contingencies* and mere *possibilities* be assigned to a stranger ? 290.
4. What seven descriptions of persons are incapable of *conveying ?* 290—293.
5. Are the *conveyances* and *purchases* of *idiots* and *persons of nonsane memory, infants,* and *persons under duress,* void. 291.
6. May a *non compos* plead his own disability, in order to avoid his acts ? 291, 292.
7. May his next heir, or other person interested, plead it ? 292.
8. How may the *purchase* of a *feme-covert* be *avoided ?* 293.

CHAP. XX.

Of Alienation by Deed.

13. What was the origin of *express warranties?* 301.

14. What was the difference between *lineal* and *collateral warranty?* 301, 302.

15. What was a *warranty commencing by disseisin?* 302.

16. In case the *warrantee* was evicted, what was the obligation of the *heir?* 302.

17. What *warranties* against the *heir* are now good? 302, 303.

18. What are *covenants?* 304.

19. What is the difference of effect, between *covenanting* for *heirs,* and *covenanting* for *executors and administrators?* 304.

20. For what reasons has the *covenant,* in modern practice, totally superseded the *warranty?* 304.

21. Of what does the *conclusion* of a deed consist? 304.

22. Is a *deed* good, with no, or a false, *date?* 304.

23. When is it necessary to the validity of a *deed,* to read it to the *parties?* 304.

24. What if a *deed* be read falsely? 304.

25. Is it necessary to *sign* as well as *seal* a *deed?* 305, 306.

26. What is the *delivery* of a *deed;* and what is its efficacy? 307.

27. What is the difference between a *deed* and an *escrow?* 307.

28. Of what use is the *attestation* of a *deed?* 307.

29. Must the *witnesses* sign the *deed?* 307, 308.

30. By what five means, may a *deed* be avoided? 308, 309.

31. What are those *deeds* called, which are generally used in the alienation of *real estates?* 309.

32. Of what two natures are *conveyances,* as to the manner in which they receive their force and efficacy? 309.

33. Of what two kinds are *conveyances by the common law?* 309.

34. What are the six species of *original conveyances;* and what the five of *derivative?* 310.

35. What is a *feoffment?* 310.

36. What is necessary to the perfection of a *feoffment?* 311.

37. What, if an *heir* dies, before *entry* made upon his *estate?* 312.

38. By what *delivery* is a *conveyance* of a *copyhold estate* made to this day? 313.

39. What is necessary, by the common law, to be made upon every *grant* of an *estate* of *freehold,* in *hereditaments corporeal?* 314.

40. What is necessary in *leases for years?* 314.

41. Why cannot freeholds be made to commence *in futuro?* 314.

42. If a *freehold remainder* be created after, and expectant on, a *lease for years* now in being, to whom must the *livery* be made? 314, 315.

57. Is either *livery of seisin* or *entry* necessary, in order to perfect an *exchange* ? 323.

58. What is a *partition* ? 324.

59. Can a *partition* be made by *parol* only, in any case ? 324.

60. What is a *release* ? 324.

61. For what five purposes may *releases* enure ? 324, 325.

62. What is a *confirmation* ? 325, 326.

63. Why is not a *livery of seisin* necessary to a *release* or *confirmation* of lands ? 325, 326.

64. What is a *surrender* ? 326.

65. Why is not a *livery of seisin* necessary to a *surrender* ? 326.

66. What is an *assignment* ; and wherein does it differ from a *lease* ? 326, 327.

67. What is a *defeazance* ; and may it be made *after* the original conveyance ? 327.

68. What are *uses* and *trusts*, in our law ? 328.

69. Who were the *terre-tenant*, and who the *cestuy que use*, or the *cestuy que trust* ? 328.

70. What was done by the *statute of uses*, 27 Hen. VIII. c. 10. ? 332, 333.

71. In what do the *contingent* or *springing uses* of a *conveyance* differ from an *executory devise* ? 334.

72. Why, in both cases, may a *fee* be limited to take effect after a *fee* ? 334.

73. What is a *secondary*, or *shifting use* ? 335.

74. What is a *resulting use* ? 335.

75. May *uses*, originally declared, be revoked at any time, and new ones declared? 335.
76. What is the origin of *trusts*? 335, 336.
77. How do the courts now consider a *trust-estate*? 337.
78. To what *twelfth* species of *conveyance* has that by *livery of seisin* now given way? 338.
79. What *thirteenth* species of *conveyance* has been introduced by this *statute of uses*? 338.
80. What was enacted by the 27 Hen. VIII. c. 16. as to *bargains* and *sales*? 338.
81. What gave rise to the *fourteenth* species of *conveyance*; and what is its nature? 338, 339.
82. What may be added as a *fifteenth* and a *sixteenth* species of *conveyance*? 339.
83. What are the three species of *deeds* used not to *convey*, but to *charge* or *discharge* lands? 340.
84. What is an *obligation* or bond, whether *single* (*simplex obligatio,*) or *conditional*; and how is it a *charge* upon lands? 340.
85. When is the *condition* of a *bond* void: and when the *bond* itself? 340, 341.
86. On the *forfeiture* of a *bond*, what sum is recoverable? 341.
87. What is a *recognizance*; and wherein does it differ from a *bond*? 341.
88. What is a *defeazance* on a *bond*, or *recognizance*, or *judgment recovered*; and wherein does it differ from a common *conditional bond*? 342.

89. What general *registers* for *deeds, wills,* and other acts affecting *real property,* are there in England and Scotland ? 343.

———

CHAP. XXI.

Of Alienation by Matter of Record.

1. WHAT are *assurances by matter of record*? 344.
2. Of what four kinds are they? 344.
3. What are the intentions of *private acts of parliament*? 344.
4. With what cantions and preliminaries, are *private acts of parliament* made? 345.
5. In what are the *King's grants* contained? 346.
6. What is the difference between the *King's letters patent, literæ patentes,* and his *writs close, literæ clausæ*? 346.
7. In what three points does the *construction* of the *King's grants* differ from those of a *subject*? 347, 348.
8. What is a *fine* of lands and tenements ? 348.
9 What is the origin of *fines*? 349.
10. Why is a *fine* so called ? 349.
11. What is the *action of covenant,* upon which the *fine* is founded ? 350.
12. What is the *primer fine*? 350.
13. What is the *licentia concordani*? 350.

14. What is the *King's silver*, or *post fine?* 350.

15. What is the *concord*; and who is the *cognizor*, and who the *cognizee?* 350, 351.

16. How must the *acknowledgment* be made; and how far does this *acknowledgment* complete the *fine?* 351.

17. What is the *note* of the *fine?* 351.

18. What is the *foot* of the *fine?* 351.

19. What *proclamations* of a *fine* hath the statute added, to prevent the *levying* of one by fraud or *covin?* 352.

20. Of what four kinds are *fines* thus *levied?* 352, 353.

21. What is a *fine sur cognizance de droit, come ceo que il ad de son done;* and of what efficacy is it? 352.

22. What is a *fine, sur cognizance de droit tantum;* and for what is it commonly used? 353.

23. What is a *fine, sur concessit?* 353.

24. What is a *fine, sur done, grant, et render;* and wherein does it differ from the *fine, sur cognizance de droit, come ceo,* &c.? 353.

25. What are the force and effect of *fines?* 354, 355.

26. What are the three classes of persons bound by a *fine?* 355.

27. Who are the *parties* to a *fine;* and how are they bound? 355.

28. Who are *privies*; and how are they bound? 355.

29. Who are *strangers*; and in what cases are they bound ?   356.

30. But what is necessary, in order to make a *fine* of any avail at all ?   356, 357.

31. Upon what neglect of the *remainder-man*, or *reversioner*, does a *tenant's for life levying a fine* fail to forfeit the *estate* from the latter to the former, and *bar* it for ever ?   356.

32. What is the nature of a *common recovery*; and how far is it like a *fine* ?   357.

33. What is the *writ of precipœ quod reddat*; and what does it allege ?   3.58.

34. Who is the *demandant*; and who the *defendant* ?   358.

35. What is the *voucher, vocatio,* or *calling to warranty*; and who is the *vouchee* ?   358.

36. Who is the *recoverer*; and who the *recoveree* ?   358.

37. What is called the *recompence,* or *recovery in value* ?   359.

38. Of what nature is this *recompence*; and who is usually the *common vouchee* ?   3.59.

39. What is a *recovery* with *double voucher*; and why is it now usually employed ?   359.

40. What is the reason, why the *issue in tail* is held to be *barred* by a *common recovery* ?   360.

41. In what light have our modern *courts of justice* considered *common recoveries* ?   360.

42. How does the commentator recommend the shortening of the process of this *conveyance* ?   361.

CHAP. XXII.

Of Alienation by special Custom.

3. What is *surrender, sursem, redditio ;* and what is the manner of transferring *copyhold estates ?* 365, 366.

4. What operation upon a *copyhold estate* has any *feoffment* or *grant ?* 367.

5. If I would exchange a *copyhold estate* with another, or devise one, what must be done? 367, 368.

6. What effect will a *fine* or *recovery,* had of *copyhold lands* in the *King's courts,* have ; and how may such *fine* or *recovery* be reversed by the *lord ?* 368.

7. What are the three several parts of the *assurance* by *surrender ?* 368.

8. What part of it does the *surrender* itself constitute ? 368.

9. What, if the *lord* refuse to *admit* the *surrenderee ?* 368.

10. Can the *surrenderor* retract his *surrender ?* 369.

11. What is the *presentment* of the *surrender ;* and when and by whom must it be presented ? 369.

12. What, if those into whose hands the *surrender* was made refuse to *present,* and the *lord* refuse to compel them to do so ? 369.

13. Of what three sorts is *admittance ?* 370.

14. What is the *lord* bound to do, in *admittance* upon a *voluntary grant ?* 370.

15. How is the *lord* regarded in *admittances upon surrender of a former tenant,* or *upon descent from the ancestor ?* 370, 371.
16. In what, however, do *admittances upon surrender* differ from *admittances upon descent ?* 371.
17. Are *heirs* of *copyhold* compellable to be *admitted ?* 372.

CHAP. XXIII.

Of Alienation by Devise.

1. WHAT is *devise?* 373.
2. Upon what did the restraint of *devising lands* take place *?* 373.
3. What *estate* only could then be *devised,* with what exceptions ? 374.
4. In what shape did the popish clergy, who then generally sat in the *Court of Chancery,* allow of the *devise* of *lands?* 375.
5. Upon what did *lands,* in this shape, become no longer *deviseable ?* 375.
6. What did the *statute of Wills,* 32 Hen. VIII c. 1., enact ? 375.
7. How is a *devise* to a *corporation,* for a charitable use, now held by the statue 43 Eliz. c. 4. to be valid ? 376.

8. What does the *statute of frauds and perjuries,* 29 Car. Car. II. c. 3., direct, as to *devises* of *lands?* 376.

9. Are *copyholds* and *terms* for *years* within the statute? To be answered from Mr. J. Christian's note (2) on this chapter. 376.

10. How may a *will* be *revoked?* 376.

11. What did the statute 25 Geo. II. c. 6. declare, as to the *witnesses* to a *will?* 377.

12. What hath the statute 3 & 4 W. & M. c. 14. provided for the benefit of a testator's creditors? 378.

13. How is a *will* of *lands* considered by the *courts of law?* 378.

14. What distinction, between *devises* of *lands* and *testaments* of *personal chattels,* is founded upon this notion? 378, 379.

15. What seven general rules and maxims have been laid down by *courts of justice* for the construction and exposition of all the species of *common assurances?* 379—382.

CHAP. XXIV.

Of Things personal.

1. WHAT are included under the name of *things personal?* 384.

2. Do not things *personal* consist of *things moveable* only, as *things real* do of *things immoveable?* 385.

3. Under what general name, then, is the whole comprehended ? 385.

4. Into what two kinds, therefore, are *chattels* distributed by the law ? 386.

5. What are *chattels real?* 386.

6. Which quality of *real estates* have they, which denominates them *real?* and which do they want, the want of which constitutes them *chattels?* 386.

7. What are *chattels personal?* 387, 888.

CHAP. XXV.

Of Property in Things personal.

1. Of what two natures is *property in chattels personal?* 389.

2. Into what two sorts is *property in chattels personal*, of the former nature, divided ? 389.

3. What is *property in chattels personal, in possession absolute?* 389.

4. Into what two classes does the law distinguish *animals?* 390.

5. What property can a man have in such animals as are *domitiæ*, and what in such as are *feræ naturæ?* 390.

6. Why, of all tame and domestic animals, does the *brood* belong to the *mother* (with what exception)? 390.

7. What is *property in chattels personal, in possession qualified, limited, or special?* 391.

8. On what three accounts may a *qualified property* subsist in *animals feræ naturæ?* 391.

9. What are those animals *feræ naturæ*, in which a *qualified property* may be acquired *per industriam hominis*, by a man's *reclaiming* and making them tame, by art, industry, and education? 392.

10. How long are these *animals* the *property* of a man? 392.

11. What *animals* is it *felony* to *steal?* 393.

12. What *crime* is it to *steal* such *animals*, the *stealing* of which, does not amount to *felony?* 394.

13. When, and how long, may a *qualified property* also subsist, with relation to *animals feræ naturæ, ratione impotentiæ*, on account of their own inability? 394.

14. What is that *qualified property*, which a man may have in *animals feræ naturæ, propter privilegium?* 394, 395.

15. What other things, besides *animals feræ naturæ*, may be the objects of *qualified property;* and how long does that *property* last? 395.

16. These kinds of *qualification* in *property* arise from the *subject's incapacity of absolute ownership*; but, in what cases, may *property* be of a *qualified* or *special* nature, on account of *the peculiar circumstances of the owner*, when the thing itself is very capable of absolute ownership? 396.

17. Hath a *servant* who hath the care of his *master's goods* or *chattels*, any *property* in them? 396.

18. What is called a *thing*, or *chose in action*? 396, 397.

19. Upon what depends, and what are the only regular means of acquiring all *property in action*? 397.

20. Upon all *contracts*, what does the law give to the *party* injured, in case of *non-performance*? 397.

21. May *things personal* be limited, by *deed* or *will* in *remainder*, and in *estate tail*? 398.

22. May *things personal* be vested in *joint-tenancy*, in *common*, and in *coparcenary*? 399.

23. But how is it held, that *partnership stock in trade* shall always be considered? 399.

CHAP. XXVI.

Of Title to Things personal by Occupancy.

1. WHAT are the twelve principal methods by which the *title to things personal* may be acquired and lost? 400.
2. In what eight species of *goods* may a *property* be acquired by *occupancy?* 401—406.
3. But what are the restrictions, as to the right to seize the *goods* and *person* of an *alien enemy?* 401, 402.
4. To what do the restrictions, which are laid upon the right to the *occupancy* of *animals feræ naturæ*, principally relate? 403.
5. What constitutes an *accession* to *property?* 404, 405.
6. What is *confusion* of goods; and to whom does such act of *confusion* give the entire *property?* 405.
7. What hath the statute declared as to *literary*, and other *copyright?* 407.

CHAP. XXVII.

Of Title by Prerogative and Forfeiture.

1. WHAT *personal chattels* may accrue to whom, by *prerogative?* 408.

2. What if the *titles* of the *King* and the *subject* concur?   409.

3. In what three classes of *books* hath the *King* a kind of *prerogative copyright*?   410.

4. Is there not still another species of *prerogative property*, founded upon a very different principle, from any that have been mentioned before?   410, 411.

5. What four reasons have concurred for making the restrictions, which the municipal laws of many nations have exerted upon the natural right of every man, to pursue, and take to his own use, all such creatures as are *feræ naturæ?*   411, 412.

6. What, however, is the origin of the *game-laws* in England?   413—416.

7. What was done by the *carta de foresta?*   416.

8. Who only, by *common law*, have a right to take or kill any *beasts of chase*, not also *beasts of prey?*   416.

9. What are *free-warren*, and *free-fishery ;* and what does *magna carta* provide as to the latter ?   417.

10. Who only, by *common-law*, can justify *hunting* or *sporting* upon another man's *soil*, or, in thorough strictness, *hunting* or *sporting* at all ?   417.

11. But how have the exemptions from certain *penal statutes* for *preserving the game* vir-

tually extended what are called the *qualifications* to kill it?   417, 418.

12. For what twelve *offences*, are all the *goods* and
chattels of the *offender forfeited* to the *crown* ?
421.

13. When do these *forfeitures commence* ?   421.

CHAP. XXVIII.

Of Title by Custom.

1. WHAT are the three sorts of *customary interests*, which obtain pretty generally throughout most parts of the nation ?   422.

2. Into what two sorts are *heriots* usually divided ?   422.

3. What is *heriot-service* ?   422.

4. Upon what does *heriot-custom* arise ; and what
is it defined to be ?   422.

5. To what species of *tenures* is *heriot-custom*
now, for the most part, confined ?   423.

6. Of what does the *heriot* now usually consist ;
and of what *estate* is it always ?   424.

7. Why can no *heriot* be taken on the death of a
feme-covert ?   424.

8. Can a *heriot* be compounded for, by the payment of *money* ?   424.

15

CHAP. XXIX.

Of Title by Succession, Marriage, and Judgment.

5. How are those *chattels* which formerly belonged to the *wife*, vested in the *husband*, by *marriage;* and how does *personal property* differ, in this respect, from *real estate ?*   4 33.

6. How do a *chattel real* and a *chattel personal*, or *chose in action*, vest in the *husband ;* and what, if he die before he have recovered, or reduced them into possession ?   434.

7. What shall become of the *chattel real* and *chattel personal*, if the *wife* die before the husband have done so ; and why ?   435.

8. How do *chattels personal in possession* vest in the husband ?   435.

9. What are the *wife's paraphernalia ?*   435, 436.

10. Of what two natures is *property in chattel interests*, vested by a *judgment*, in consequence of some *suit* or *action ?*   436, 437.

11. What three species of *property* are of the second of these natures ?   437—439.

CHAP. XXX.

Of Title by Gift, Grant, and Contract.

1. WHAT is the distinction between a *gift* of *personal property*, and a *grant ?*   440.

2. What may be included under the head of *gifts or grants of chattels real;* and *what considera-*

tions, in the eye of the law, convert the *gift,* if executed, into a *grant,* if not executed, into a *contract?* 440.

3. What are *grants* or *gifts* of *chattels personal;* and how may they be made ? 441.

4. Why does the statute 3 Hen. VII. c. 4. declare all *deeds of gifts* of *goods,* made in trust to the use of the donor, void ; and what does the statute 13 Eliz. c. 5. declare, as to every *grant* or *gift* of *chattels,* as well as lands, with intent to defraud creditors ? 441.

5. By what is a true and proper *gift* or *grant* always accompanied ; and in what cases only may it be retracted ? 441.

6. But what if the *gift* do not take effect, by delivery of immediate possession ? 441, 442.

7. What *interest* does a *contract* convey, as distinguished from a *gift* or *grant;* and how is it defined ? 442.

8. Can a *chose in action* be *assigned?* 442.

9. What are *express contracts,* and what *implied?* 443.

10. What are *executed,* and what *executory contracts ;* and how do they differ in the *choses* they *convey?* 443.

11. What is a *good,* and what a *valuable, consideration ;* and how may each of these be *set aside ?* 444.

12. Into what four species are *valuable considerations* divided, by the *civilians?* 444, 445.

13. What is a *nudum pactum?* and what degree of *reciprocity* will prevent it? 445, 446.
14. How far will *courts of justice* support a *voluntary bond*, or *promissory note*; and why? 446.
15. What are the four most usual *contracts* whereby the *right* of *chattels personal* may be acquired in England? 446.
16. What is *sale* or *exchange;* how does the former differ from the latter; and how are both regarded by the law? 416, 447.
17. Where the *vendor* hath in himself the *property* of the *goods*, when only hath he not the liberty of disposing of them? 417.
18. What constitutes a *sale?* 447, 448.
19. But in what cases may *property* be transferred by *sale*, though the *vendor* have none at all in the *goods?* 449.
20. What is *market-day*, and *market-overt* in the *country;* and what in *London?* 449.
21. But what has the statute 1 Jac. I. c. 21. provided, as to the *sale* of *goods* to *pawn brokers?* 449.
22. And in what cases are *sales* not binding. even in *market-overt?* 450.
23. What directions do the statutes, 2 P. & M. c. 7., and 31 Eliz. c. 12., enact concerning the *sale* of *horses?* 450, 451.
24. What remedy has a *purchaser*, if a *vendor* sell *goods* and *chattels* as his own, and the *title* prove deficient? 451.

25. When is the *vendor* bound to answer for the goodness of his wares purchased ? 451.

26. What is *bailment;* and who is the *bailor,* and who the *bailee ?* 451, 452.

27. What does the law call *agistment ?* 452.

28. If a man deliver any thing to his friend to keep for him, when is the *bailee* answerable for any damage or loss it may sustain ? 452.

29. Why, in all instances of *bailment,* may the *bailee,* as well as the *bailor,* maintain an *action* against such as injure the *chattels* *bailed ?* 452, 453.

30. What is the difference between *hiring* and *borrowing ?* 453.

31. What is *interest;* and upon what is its doctrines grounded ? 454, 455.

32. To what three practices does the circumstance of the hazard of *lending money* being greater than the compensation arising from the rate of *interest* allowed by law on the *loan,* give rise ? 457.

33. What is *bottomry ;* and in what does it differ from *respondentia ?* 457, 458.

34. What is enacted by the statute 19 Geo. II. c. 37. as to all monies lent on *bottomry* or *respondentia,* on vessels bound to and from the West Indies ? 458.

35. What is a *policy of insurance?* 458, 459.

36. What is enacted by the statute 14 Geo. III. c. 48. as to *insurances on lives ?* 459, 460.

37. *Policies of insurance* being *contracts*, the very essence of which consists in observing the purest good faith and integrity, how is fraud or undue concealment in them provided against ? 460.

38. What is enacted by the statute 19 Geo. II. c. 37. as to what are denominated *wagering policies ?* 460, 461.

39. From what does the practice of purchasing *annuities for lives* at a certain price or *premium*, instead of advancing the same sum on an ordinary *loan*, arise ? 461.

40. What has the statute 37 Geo. III. c. 26. directed, in order to throw some check upon improvident transactions of this kind ? 461, 462.

41. What is now the extremity of *legal interest* that can be taken ? 463.

42. If a *contract* which carries interest, be made in a foreign country, of what *interest* will our *courts* direct the payment ? 463, 464.

43. What does the statute 14 Geo. III. c. 79. enact, as to the *legality* of *interest* on all *mortgages*, and other *securities* upon *estates*, or other *property* in *Ireland*, or the *plantations ?* 464.

44. What is *debt ;* and in what cases may it be the counterpart of, and arise from any of the other species of *contracts ?* 464.

45. Into what three classes is *debt* usually divided ? 465.

46. What is a *debt of record ?* 465.

47. What is a *debt by specialty,* or *special contract?* 465.

48. What are *debts by simple contract?* 465.

49. What is enacted by the statute 29 Car. II. c. 3. as to one person's being responsible for the *debt* of another? 466.

50. What is that species of *simple contract debt* now introduced into all sorts of *civil* life, under the name of *paper credit?* 466.

51. What is a *bill of exchange* or *draft;* and who is the *drawer* of it, who the *drawee,* and who the *payee?* 466, 467.

52. Of what two sorts are *bills of exchange;* and what difference is there in law between them? 467.

53. What are *promissory notes,* or *notes of hand,* and for what sum at least must they be drawn? 467, 468.

54. Why is it usual in *bills of exchange,* to express that the *value* thereof hath been *received* by the *drawer?* 468.

55. By what means may a *bill of exchange,* or *promissory note,* be assigned? 468, 469.

56. When may a *bill of exchange* be *protested* for *non-acceptance;* and when, both a *bill* and a *promissory note,* for *non-payment?* 469.

57. In case of such *protests,* what compensation is the *drawer* bound to make to the *payee* or *indorsee;* but what happens in the absence of such *protests,* or their *notification* to the *drawer?* 469.

58. When a *bill* or a *note* is *refused*, how soon must it be demanded of the *drawer?* 470.

59. Upon whom may an *indorsee* call to *discharge* a *bill* or a *note?* 4.0.

———

CHAP. XXXI.

Of Title by Bankruptcy.

1. WHO may become a *bankrupt;* and who may not? 471, 473—477.

2. What privileges do the laws of *bankruptcy* confer on the *creditors;* and what on the *debtor?* 472.

3 By what eleven acts, may a man become a *bankrupt?* 478, 479.

4. What are the ten *proceedings* on a *commission of bankrupt?* 480—484.

5. What, if the *bankrupt* make default in either surrender of himself, or conformity to the directions of the statutes of *bankruptcy?* 481.

6. What powers has any *judge* or *justice of the peace* over a *bankrupt?* 481.

7. What powers have the *commissioners* of the bankruptcy? 481.

8. What, if the *bankrupt* conceal or embezzle any *effects* to the amount of 20l., or withhold

16

any books or writings, with intent to defraud
his creditors ? 482.

9. What if it appear that his inability to pay his
debts arose from some gross misconduct and
negligence? 482.

10. After the time allowed to the *bankrupt* for
such discovery is expired, to what shall any
other person, voluntarily discovering any
part of the *bankrupt's estate*, be entitled;
and what shall any *trustee*, wilfully concealing it, forfeit? 482.

11. Of what rateable amount is the *bankrupt's
allowance?* 483.

12. When shall not the *bankrupt's allowance* or
indemnity be given him? 484.

13. What is an *act of insolvency?* 484.

14. But as to what only, are persons, who have
been once cleared by a *bankruptcy,* or by an
insolvent act, indemnified, in case they become *bankrupts* again? 484, 485.

15. By virtue of the statutes of *bankruptcy,* in
whom are all the *personal estate* and *effects*
of the *bankrupt* considered as vested, by the
act of bankruptcy? 485.

16. What is the meaning of the saying, " *Once
a bankrupt, and always a bankrupt?*" 485,
486.

17. Who alone is not within the statute of *bankrupts?* 486.

18. But what is provided by the statute 19 Geo. II. c. 32. as to money paid by a *bankrupt* to a *creditor*, and by statute 1 Jac. 1. c. 15. as to money paid by a *debtor* to a *bankrupt*? 486.

19. What acts can and cannot the *assignees* of a *bankrupt* do, without the consent of the *creditors*? 486.

20. What is the duty of the *assignees* towards the *creditors*; and within what time shall the first dividend be made? 487.

21. What *debts* of a *bankrupt* have a priority to be paid; and what shall not be postponed or set aside? 487, 488.

22. Within what time shall a second and final *dividend* be made; and if any *surplus* remain after paying every *creditor* his full *debt*, to whom shall it be given? 488.

CHAP. XXXII.

Of Title by Testament, and Administration.

1. WHAT is a *testament*, and what an *administration*? 490.

2. What were the *reasonable parts* in a man's *chattels* of the *wife* and *children*? 492.

3. What part of his *chattels* may a man now *devise*? 492, 493.

4. When is a man said to die *intestate?*   494.

5. To whom did the *goods* of *intestates* antiently belong ; and to whom were they granted ? 494.

6. What is the origin of the right of the *church* to the *probate* of *wills*, and to the *administration* of *intestate's property?*   494—496, 509, 510.

7. Who is the *intestate's administrator ?*   496.

8. Upon what three accounts are persons prohibited, by law or custom, from making a will ? 497.

9. Who are to be reckoned in the first species ? 497.

10. Are *prisoners, captives*, and the like, absolutely *intestable?*   497.

11. In what cases may a *feme-covert* make a *testament* of *chattels ?*   498.

12. Who is an exception to the general rule, that a *feme-covert* cannot make a *testament* of *chattels ?*   498.

13. What, if a *feme-sole* make her will, and afterwards marry ?   499.

14. Who are persons incapable of making *testaments*, on account of their criminal conduct ? 499.

15. Into what two sorts are *testaments* divided ? 500.

16. What is a *codicil;* and of what two sorts ; 500.

17. Under what three restrictions has the *statute of frauds*, 29 Car. II. c. 3. laid *nuncupative wills* and *codicils ?* 500, 501.

18. What *witness* of their *publication* do *written testaments* of *chattels* need ? 501.

19. What if there be many *testaments* of different dates ; and what effect has the *republication* of a former *will* upon one of a later date ? 502.

20. In what three ways may *testaments* be avoided ? 502.

21. What, if a man who hath made a *will*, marry, and have a child ? 502.

22. Is it necessary to leave the *heir* a *shilling ;* or, if the *heir* or *next of kin* be totally omitted in the *will*, does the law admit a *querela inofficiosi* to set it aside ? 503.

23. What is an *executor ;* and who may be one ? 503.

24. What must be done, if the *executor* be not seventeen years of age, or be out of the realm, or when a *suit* is commenced in the *ecclesiastical court* touching the validity of the *will !* 503.

25. What, if the testator name no, or incapable, *executors ;* or if the *executors* named, refuse to act ? 503, 504.

26. What, if the deceased die wholly *intestate*, without making either *will* or *executors ?* 504.

27. In granting *letters of administration* pursuant to the statutes 31 Edw. III. c. 11., and 21 Hen. VIII. c. 5. by what seven rules is the *ordinary* bound ?   504, 505.

28. Who may *administer* to a *bastard* ?   505, 506.

29. If the *executor* of A. die, who is A's *executor?*   506.

30. Is it the same, with regard to A's *administrator?*   506.

31. What is an *administrator de bonis non* ?   506.

32. What is the difference between the offices and duties of *executors* and those of *administrators* ?   507.

33. Who is an *executor de son tort*; and how shall he be treated ?   507.

34. What are the seven powers and duties of a rightful *executor* or *administrator* ?   508, 510 —512. 514, 515.

35. In what two ways is a *will proved*; and what is styled the *probate* ?   508.

36. When must the will be *proved* before the *ordinary* of the *jurisdiction* and when before the *metropolitan* of the *province*, by way of *special prerogative* ?   508, 509.

37. If there be two or more *executors* or *administrators*, is a *sale* or *release* by one of them good against the rest?   510.

38. What are called *assets* ?   510.

39. In what order of priority must the deceased's *debts* be paid? 511.

40. What, if a *creditor* constitute his *debtor* his *executor*? 512.

41. May an *executor* or *administrator* give himself the preference in the payment of the deceased's *debts* and *legacies*? 511, 512.

42. What is a *legacy*; and what is necessary to its perfection? 512.

43. In case of a deficiency of assets, what *legacies* must *abate*, and how? 512, 513.

44. What is a *lapsed legacy*; and to whom does it *lapse*? 513.

45. What is a *contingent*, and what a *vested, legacy*? 513.

46. But what, if such *legacies* be charged upon *real estate*? 513.

47. When do *legacies* carry *interest*? 513, 514.

48. What is a *donation causa mortis*? 514.

49. When shall the *residuum* go to the *executor*, and when to the *next of kin*? 514, 515.

50. How do the statutes 22 & 23 Car. II. c. 10., explained by 29 Car. II. c. 30., and 1 Jac. II. c. 17., distribute the surplusage of *intestates'* *estates*? 515, 516.

51. But what are the *customs* of the *city* of *London*, and the *province* of *York*, as to the distribution of *intestate's effects*, which are expressly reserved by the *statute of distributions*? 518, 519.

52. What is the *widow's chamber*, by these *customs?* 518.

53 What was the *dead man's part?* 518.

54. In what two principal points, do the *customs* of *London* and *York* considerably differ? 519.

BOOK THE THIRD.

OF PRIVATE WRONGS.

―――

CHAP. 1.

Of the Redress of private Wrongs, by the mere Act of the Parties.

1. WHAT are *private wrongs*, as distinguished from *public wrongs ;* and why are the former frequently termed *civil injuries*, and the latter *crimes* and *misdemeanors ?*   2.

2. How is the redress of *private wrongs* principally to be sought ?   2, 3.

3. Into what three species, may the redress of *private wrongs* be distributed?   3.

4. Of what two sorts is that redress of *private wrongs*, which is obtained by the mere *act* of the *parties ?*   3.

5. Of what six species, is that redress of *private wrongs*, which arises from the *sole act* of the *injured party ?*   3—6. 15.

17

6. What is a *distress, districtio;* and for what four *injuries* may a *distress* be taken ? 6, 7.

7. What are *cattle, damage-feasant?* 7.

8. What six species of *things* cannot be *distrained?* 7—10.

9. What are cattle, *levant* and *couchant elevantes et cubantes ?* 9.

10. When, where, and how, must all *distresses* be made ; with what exceptions as to the time ? 11.

11. In what cases, may a second *distress* for the same *duty* be made ? 11, 12.

12. What does the *statute of Marlbridge,* 52 H. III. c. 4. enact as to *unreasonable distress ?* 12.

13. How must a *distress* be disposed of ; and when may it be *rescued* by its owner ? 12.

14. What is a *pound (parcus) ;* and of what four kinds ? 12.

15. What is the difference in the effect, between *impounding* a *live distress* in a *common pound-overt*, and in a *special pound-overt?* 13.

16. What, if the *beasts* are put in a *pound-covert ;* or, if a *distress* of *dead chattels* be not put in one ? 13.

17. How long must *beasts* taken *damage-feasant.* and *distresses* for *suit* or *services*, remain *impounded ?* 13.

18. What is to *replevy (replegiare)?* 13.

19. When is the *distress* saleable, for a *debt* due to the *crown*, for an *amercement* to the *lord.*

and for *statute distresses;* and when in all cases of *distress* for *rent?* 14.

20. What has the statute 11 Geo. II. c. 19. provided in case of any unlawful act, done in taking a *distress?* 15.

21. Are those who are entitled to that redress of *private wrongs,* which arises from the *sole act* of the *injured party,* debarred of their redress by *suit* or *action?* 15.

22. Of what two species, is that redress of *private wrongs* which arises from the *joint act* of *all the parties* together? 15.

23. What is *accord;* and what is its effect? 15, 16.

24. In what cases, is *tender* of sufficient amends to the *party injured,* a *bar* of all *actions?* 16.

25. What is *arbitration;* who is an *umpire (imperator* or *impar);* and what is an *award?* 16.

26. How may the right of *real property* pass by an *award?* 16.

27. In what case does the statute 9 & 10 W. III. c. 15. enact, that all submissions of *suit* to *arbitration* or *umpirage,* may be made *rules* of any of the *King's courts of record?* 17.

CHAP. II.

Of redress by the mere Operation of Law.

1. Of what two species is that redress of *private wrongs*, which is effected by the *mere operation of law?*   18.
2. Why, when a *creditor* is *executor* or *administrator*, is he allowed to *retain* his own *debt?* 18, 19.
3. But in prejudice to whom, can he not *retain* his own *debt?*   19.
4. What is *remitter?*   19, 20.
5. But what if the subsequent *estate*, or *right of possession*, be gained by a man's own act and consent?   20.
6. What is the reason why this remedy of *remitter* to a *right* was allowed?   20.
7. But what, too, if the party have no remedy by *action?*   21.

———

CHAP. III.

Of Courts in general.

1. WHAT is that redress of *private wrongs*, wherein the *act of the parties* and the *act of law* co-operate?   22.

2. Is not the ordinary course of *justice* excluded by the extra-judicial remedy, which the law allows, in the several cases of redress by the *act of the parties*, mentioned in a former chapter ? 22, 23.

3. What, in the cases of remedy by the mere *operation of law* ? 23.

4. What is a general and indisputable rule, where there is a legal *right* ? 23.

5. What is a *court* defined to be ? 23.

6. Whence are all *courts of justice* derived ? 24.

7. What one distinction runs throughout all *courts of justice* ? 24.

8. What constitutes a *court of record*; and by what shall its existence be tried ? 24, 25.

9. What is a *court not of record*; what is the extent of its power ; and by what shall its existence be tried ? 25.

10. What three constituent parts must there be, in every *court*; and what assistants is it usual for the *superior courts* to have ? 25.

11. What is an *attorney at law*? 25.

12. Who cannot appear in *court* by *attorney* ? 25.

13. What are the qualifications of *attornies* ? 26.

14. Of what two species, or degrees, are *advocates*, or *counsel*? 26.

15. When may a *barrister* be called to the state and degree of a *serjeant*; and who are, by custom, always admitted into this venerable order, as a qualification for their office ? 27.

CHAP. IV.

Of the public Courts of Common Law, and Equity.

throughout the whole kingdom, which are *courts* of *record*, and which *not*, and which are *courts* of *equity* as well as *law ?* 32—35. 37. 41. 44. 47, 48. 56, 57.

4. What is the *court of piepoudre;* who is the *judge* of it ; what is its jurisdiction ; and where lies an appeal from it *?* 32, 33.

5. What is the *court-baron;* by whom is it held as *registrar;* and of what two natures is it *?* 33.

6. Before whom, as *judges,* is the *court-baron* of the second, or *common-law,* nature held ; what *pleas* may it hold ; whither may its *proceedings* be removed ; and where lies an appeal from it *?* 34.

7. What is a *hundred-court;* who are its *judges* and *registrar;* whither may its *proceedings* be removed ; and where lies an appeal from it *?* 34, 35.

8. What is the *country-court;* what *pleas* may it hold ; who are its real *judges,* and who its *ministerial officer;* whither may its *proceedings* be removed ; and where lies an appeal from it *?* 36, 37.

9. What is the origin of the *court of common pleas* or *common bench ;* and by what was the *court* rendered fixed and stationary, where *?* 38, 39.

10. What benefit did the *common law* itself derive from this establishment of its principal *court ?* 39.

11. Into what two sorts, are *pleas* or *suits* regular-
ly divided ; and of what *court's* jurisdiction
were each of these the proper objects ? 40.

12.   What are the *judges* of the *court of common
pleas ;* and when do they sit ?   41.

13. Where lies an appeal from this *court ?*   41.

14. What is the *court of King's bench ;* why is it
so called, and what are its *judges ?*   41.

15. For what reason, is all *process* issuing out of
this *court* in the *King's* name, returnable
" *ubicunque fuerimus in Anglia?*"   41, 42.

16. What is the jurisdiction of this *court ;* and, by
what fiction, can it hold *plea* of all personal
actions whatever ?   42—44.

17. Where lies an appeal from this *court ?*   44.

18. What is the court of *exchequer (scaccharium) ;*
why is it so called ; and what is its rank ? 44.

19. Of what two divisions does it consist; and
what are the two subdivisions of the second
division ?   44.

20. Where, and before whom is the *exchequer
court of equity* held ; and what is the primary
and original business of this *court ?*   45

21. But by what fiction, with the help of the
common law part of this *court's* jurisdiction,
may all kinds of *personal suits* be prosecuted
in it ?   45, 46.

22. Where lies an appeal from the *equity* side of
this court ; and where from the *common law ?*
46.

23. What is the *court of chancery (cancellaria)*; why is it so called; and how is the office of *chancellor* or *lord keeper*, created? 47.

24. What is the *chancellor virtute officii*; and what are his powers and authorities? 47, 48.

25. Of what two distinct tribunals does the *court of chancery* consist? 48.

26. What is the jurisdiction of the ordinary *legal court* in *chancery*; what, if any *fact* be disputed between the *parties*; and where lies an appeal from its *judgments in law?* 48, 49.

27. What *writs* issue from the *common law court* in *chancery*; and what is the origin of the *hanaper* and *petty bag* offices? 49.

28. What is the origin of the separate jurisdiction of the *chancery*, as a *court of equity?* 51— 53.

29. How was that notable dispute decided which was set on foot by Sir Edward Coke, when *chief justice* of the *court of King's bench*, whether a *court of equity* could give relief after, or against a *judgment* at the *common law?* 54.

30. What *chancellor* first built a system of *equitable* jurisprudence and jurisdiction upon wide and rational foundations, and occasioned the power and business of the *court* of *chancery*, to increase to its present amazing degree? 56.

31. Where lies an appeal from this *court of equity* in *chancery*; and what two differences are

18

there between *appeals* from a *court of equity,*
and *writs of error* from a *court of law?*   56.

32. What is the nature of all the branches of the
    court of exchequer chamber; and of whom
    does it now consist?   56, 57.

33. Where lies an appeal from this *court?*   57.

34. What is the nature of the *house of peers* as a
    court of judicature; and where lies an appeal
    from it?   57.

35. What is an *eleventh* species of *courts,* of gene-
    ral jurisdiction and use, which are derived out
    of, and act as collateral auxiliaries to, the
    foregoing?   58.

36. Of what are these *courts* composed; how
    often in the year are they instituted; and for
    what purpose?   58, 59.

37. By virtue of what five several authorities
    do the *judges* upon their *circuits* now sit?
    60.

38. What is a commission *of assise?*   60.

39. What is a commission of *nisi prius?*   60,

CHAP. V.

Of Courts ecclesiastical, military, and maritime.

1. WHO first separated the *ecclesiastical court*
   from the *civil?*   62.

2. What are the seven principal *courts* of *ecclesi-astical* jurisdiction, or as they are often styled, *courts Christian (curiæ Christiani-tatis)*, beginning with the lowest ? 64—67.

3. What is the jurisdiction of the *archdeacon's court;* before whom may it be held ; and where lies an appeal from it? 64.

4. What is the jurisdiction of the *consistory court* of every *diocesan bishop?* where is it held ; who is the *judge;* and where lies an appeal from it ? 64.

5. What is the *court of arches;* why is its *judge* called *dean of the arches ;* what is now the ju-risdiction of the *court;* and where lies an ap-peal from it ? 64, 65.

6. What is the *court of peculiars;* what is its ju-risdiction ; and where lies an appeal from it ? 65.

7. What is the jurisdiction of the *prerogative court;* by whom is the judge appointed ; and where lies an appeal from it ? 65, 66.

8. What is the nature of the *court of delegates (judices delegati)*; and by whom are they ap-pointed ? 66, 67.

9. What is a *commission of review?* 67.

10. What is the only *court military* known to, and established by, the permanent laws of the land ; before whom is it held ; of what has it cognizance; and where lies an appeal from it? 68.

11. What are the three *maritime courts*; and what are their power and jurisdiction ? 68, 69.

12. Before whom is the *court of admiralty* held ; according to the method of what law are its proceedings ; and where is it held ? 69.

13. Where lies an appeal from the ordinary sentences of the *admiralty judge* ; but, in cases of *prize vessels* taken in time of war in any part of the world and condemned in any of the *courts of admiralty* or *vice-admiralty* as lawful prize, where lies an appeal ? 69.

━━

CHAP. VI.

Of Courts of a Special Jurisdiction.

1. WHAT are the ten *courts*, whose jurisdiction is *private* and special, confined to particular spots, or instituted only to redress particular injuries ? 71. 73—75. 77—80. 83.

2. What were the *forest-courts* ? 71—73.

3. By whom is the *court* of *commissioners of sewers* appointed ; what are their jurisdiction and power ; and under whose control are they ? 73, 74.

4. What are the power and jurisdiction of the *court* of *policies of assurance* ; by whom may it be appointed ; of whom does it consist ; and why has it fallen into disuse ? 74, 75.

5. What is the origin of the *court* of the *marshal-sea*, and the *palace-court* at Westminster; how were both revived by King Charles I. ; what is their present jurisdiction; how may their *proceedings* be removed; and where lies an appeal from them ?   75, 76.

6. What are the *courts* of the *principality of Wales;* by whom are the *judges* of *session* appointed ; what is their jurisdiction; and where lies an appeal from their *judgments ?*   77.

7. What *writs* of *process* of the *King's courts at Westminster* run into the *principality of Wales;* and when may *actions* between Welch parties be brought in the English *courts*, and where may they be tried ?   77, 78.

8. What are the nature and jurisdiction of the *court* of the *ducy-chamber of Lancaster;* and before whom may it be held ?   78.

9. What is the jurisdiction of the *courts* appertaining to the *counties palatine* of *Chester, Lancaster,* and *Durham,* and the *royal franchise* of *Ely;* under whose *government* are these *franchises;* and by virtue of what do the *judges* of *assize* sit therein ?   78, 79.

10. What *franchises* and exclusive jurisdiction (before whom) have the *cinque ports* of *Dover, Sandwich, Romney, Hastings,* and *Hythe,* to which *Winchelsey* and *Rye* have been added; and what is the progress of an appeal from them ?   79.

11. Why may all *prerogative writs* issue to these exempt jurisdictions ?   79.

12. What are the *stannary courts* in Devonshire and Cornwall ; and before whom are they held ?   79.

13. What are the privileges of *tinners;* and what is the progress of appeal from decisions in a *stannary court ?*   80.

14. What is the origin of the several *courts* within the city of London, and other cities, boroughs, and corporations, held by prescription, charter, or act of parliament ; under what superintendancy are they ; and according to what law must their proceedings be?   80, 81.

15. What are the nature and constitution of the *courts of requests* or *courts of conscience ;* and wherein do their proceedings vary from the course of the *common law?*   81.

16. What does the commentator recommend, in preference to *courts of requests ;* and why ?   82, 83.

17. In what one instance have the proceedings in the *county* and *hundred courts* been again revived by the statute 23 Geo. III. c. 33. ; and what does it enact ?   83.

18. What are the jurisdiction and system of jurisprudence of the *chancellor's courts* in the two *universities* of England ; and why, in the reign of Queen Elizabeth, was an act of *parliament* obtained, confirming all the *charters* of the two *universities?*   83—85.

19. Who is the *judge* of the *chancellor's court;* and what is the progress of an appeal from its decisions ? *35.*

———

CHAP. VII.

Of the Cognizance of private Wrongs.

1. OF what three classes are *wrongs* or *injuries* cognizable by the *ecclesiastical court,* not for the sake of the party *injuring (pro salute animæ),* but for the sake of the party *injured ?* 87, 88.

2. From what five principal *injuries,* do the *pecuniary causes,* cognizable in the *ecclesiastical court,* arise ? 88—92.

3. When will a suit for *tithes* lie in *ecclesiastical courts?* 88, 89.

4. What, by the antient law, and by the statute 2 & 3 Edw. VI. c. 13, is the penalty, in case any person shall carry off his *predial tithes* before the tenth part be duly set forth, or agreement be made with the proprietor, or shall withdraw his *tithes* of the same, or shall hinder the proprietor of the *tithes,* or his deputy from viewing, or carrying them away ? 89.

5. But how may what *tithes* and *dues* be recover-

ed, by statutes 7 W. III. c. 6., and 8 W. III.
c. 34.? 89, 90.

6. When will a suit for *fees* lie in the *ecclesiastical courts ?*   90.

7. When has a *curate* a remedy for his salary, in the *ecclesiastical court ?*   90.

8. What is *spoliation*, and when is it cognizable in the *spiritual court?*   90, 91.

9. When will the *temporal courts* interfere with the *spiritual* in *causes matrimonial?*   93.

10. What are the four principal *matrimonial causes*, now cognizable in the *ecclesiastical courts ?*   93, 94.

11. When does the *ecclesiastical law* decree a divorce *à mensâ et thoro*, and when *à vinculo matrimonii ?*   94.

12. What are the three principal *testamentary causes*, belonging to the *ecclesiastical* jurisdiction ?   98.

13. In what cases of *testamentary causes* do the *courts of equity* exercise a concurrent jurisdiction with the *ecclesiastical courts ;* and why ?   98.

14. According to the practice of what laws, are the proceedings in the *ecclesiastical courts* regulated ?   100.

15. When will the *courts* of *common law* award a prohibition against the proceedings in the *spiritual court ?*   100.

16. What is the ordinary course of proceeding in the *ecclesiastical courts ?*   100. 101.

17. What *process* have the *ecclesiastical courts* to enforce their *sentences?* 101.

18. What are the two sorts of *excommunication?* 101.

19. What if the *judge* of any *spiritual court* excommunicate a man for a cause, of which he hath not the legal cognizance ? 101.

20. What acts is an excommunicated person disabled from doing ? 102.

21. What are writs of *significavit*, or *de excommunicato capiendo*, and *de excommunicato deliberando ;* when, and whence do they issue ; and what are their effects ? 102.

22. What assistance is given by the statutes 27 Hen. VIII. c. 20., and 32 Hen. VIII. c. 7. in case of *subtraction of tithes?* 102, 103.

23. What is the jurisdiction of the *court military*, or *courts of chivalry*, declared to be, by statute 13 Ric. II c. 2.; and, by what fiction of *common law*, has it been still more narrowly confined ? 103.

24. Of what two *civil injuries*, is it cognizable ? 103, 104.

25. Will an *action for words* lie, and what remedy can the *court military* give as a *court of honour?* 104.

26. What were the proceedings of the *court military*, as a *court of heraldry* and *precedence ;* and why has it fallen into disuse ? 105.

27. What *deeds* and *records* of the *heralds* are received as evidence in a *court of justice?* 105.

28. How has the *house of lords* provided for the *descent of peers?* 106.

29. Have the *courts maritime* cognizance of any thing done by water within the body of any *county*, of *wrecks*, of things *flotsam, jetsam,* and *ligan*, of seaman's wages contracted for on land, of *charter-parties*, or ship covenants, or of contracts made upon sea to be performed in England ; and what is the general rule as to their jurisdiction ? 106, 107.

30. By what fiction of *common law*, has the cognizance of *suits* been drawn from the *courts* of *admiralty* to those of *Westminster-hall?* 107.

31. What, if a question, that is proper for the cognizance of the *court* of *admiralty*, should arise in a *cause*, of which that *court* hath not the original jurisdiction ; or, if a question, properly determinable by the *common law*, should arise in a *cause*, of which the *court* of *admiralty* hath the original jurisdiction ? 108.

32. Upon what laws are the proceedings of the *courts of admiralty* founded ? 108.

33. What are their *process* and power ? 108, 109.

34. What *injuries* are cognizable by the *courts* of *common law?* 109.

35. What is the remedy, when *justice* is either refused or delayed by an *inferior court*, that has proper cognizance of the cause ? 109.

36. What is a writ of *procedendo ad judicium* ; and when, and whence, does it issue ? 109, 110.

37. What is a writ of *mandamus;* and when, and whence, does it issue? 110, 111.

38. What is a *peremptory mandamus;* when does it issue; and what if a *false return* should be made to it? 111.

39. What is the remedy, when an *inferior court* encroaches on its jurisdiction, or calls one *coram non judice,* to answer in a *court* that has no legal cognizance of the cause? 111.

40. What is a writ of *prohibition;* and when, whence, and whither, does it issue? 112.

41. What, if the *judge,* or the *party,* shall proceed after such *prohibition?* 113.

42. What is the usual form of proceeding upon *prohibitions?* 113.

43. When is the *party* applying for the *prohibition,* directed to *declare* in *prohibition;* and what is the nature and effect of that proceeding? 113, 114.

44. When is a writ of *consultation* awarded upon that proceeding; why is it so called; and what is its effect? 114.

45. What, if the *fact,* upon which the *prohibition* is granted, be afterwards falsified? 114.

46. In what other case, is the writ of *consultation* frequently granted? 114.

CHAP. VIII.

Of Wrongs, and their Remedies, respecting the Rights of Persons.

1. WHAT two things may be considered, in treating of the cognizance of *injuries* by the *courts* of *common law?*   115.

2. What is the plain, natural remedy for every species of *wrong*, between *subject and subject?*   116.

3. In what two ways, may this remedy be effected?   116.

4. What are the instruments, whereby this remedy is obtained ?   116.

5. Into what three kinds, are the *suits*, from the subject of them distinguished ?   117.

6. Of what two sorts, are *personal actions ;* and upon what is each said to be founded ?   117.

7. What are *real actions ;* and why, and for what, are they now pretty generally laid aside in· practice ?   118.

8. What are *mixed actions ?*   118.

9. What distinction, into two kinds, runs through all *civil injuries ;* the latter species, why savouring of the criminal kind, and how, therefore, in strictness of law, liable to a double punishment ?   118, 119.

10. May we make the same division of *injuries*, that we did of *rights* in a former book ?   119.

11. Into what two kinds, may we remember, were the *rights of persons* distributed ; and what three were the *absolute rights* of each individual defined to be ; and must the *wrongs* or *injuries* affecting them be of a correspondent nature ?   119.

12. Of what five kinds, are the *injuries*, which affect the *personal security* of individuals ? 119.

13. By what five means, may the two species of *injuries*, affecting the limbs or bodies of individuals, be committed ?   120, 121.

14. What is necessary to complete the *injury* of *threat* ?   120.

15. What constitutes *assault* ?   120.

16. What constitutes *battery ;* and when is *battery* justifiable ?   120.

17. What is the plea of *son assault demesne* ? 120.

18. What is the plea of *molliter manus imposuit ;* and when may it be pleaded in *justification* ? 121.

19. What is *mayhem* ?   121.

20. What are the *members*, the loss of which constitutes *mayhem ;* and what are not ?   121.

21. For which of these five *injuries*, may an indictment be brought, as well as an *action ;* and why ?   121.

22. What are the *injuries*, affecting a man's *health :* and, these being *injuries* unaccompanied by force, what is the remedy for them ?   122.

23. What is the special action of *trespass* or
transgression *upon the case;* and why is it
so called ? 122.

24. When is it a settled distinction, that the remedy shall be by an action of *trespass vi et
armis,* and when by an action of *trespass
upon the case?* 123.

25. Of what three kinds are *injuries,* affecting a
man's *reputation,* or good name ? 123. 125,
126.

26. What *words* are *actionable,* without proving
any particular *damage* to have happened,
but merely upon the probability that it
might happen ? 123, 124.

27. What is *scandalum magnatum ;* how is it
redressed ; and, if tending to scandalize
whom, are *words* reputed more highly injurious than ordinary ? 123, 124.

28. What is called. laying an action for *words,*
with a *per quod ?* 124.

29. When are scandals cognizable only in the
ecclesiastical court ? 124, 125.

30. What *words* are not *actionable?* 124, 125.

31. When will no *action* for *words* lie, even
though *special damage* have ensued, and is it
damnum absequœ injuriâ? 125.

32. What are *libels ;* and why are there what two
remedies for *libels?* 125.

33. In the remedy, by *action on the case,* for *libel*
may the *defendant justify* the truth of the

facts, and shew that the *plaintiff* has received no *injury* at all? 125, 126.

34. What is it necessary for the plaintiff to shew, in *actions* for *libels*, by signs and pictures? 126.

35. In the case of *injuries*, affecting a man's *reputation* by *malicious prosecutions*, when does the law give him the choice of what two remedies? 126.

36. By what *injury* is the *right* of *personal liberty* violated? 127.

37. What two points are requisite, to constitute the *injury* of *false imprisonment?* 127, 128.

38. Of what two sorts, is the remedy for *false imprisonment?* 128.

39. What are the four means of *removing* the actual *injury* of *false imprisonment?* 128.

40. What is the *writ* of *mainprize, manucaptio;* when is it *generally* granted, and when *specially;* and how do *mainpernors* differ from *bail?* 128.

41. What is the *writ de odio et atia;* what does *magna carta* say of it; by what was it abolished; and by what is Sir Edward Coke of opinion that it was revived? 128, 129.

42. What is the *writ de homine replegiando;* and when does a process issue, called a *capias in withernam;* and what is its effect? 129.

43. But what hath almost entirely antiquated these three remedies of *false imprisonment;* and to what hath it caused a general re-

course to be had, in behalf of persons thus aggrieved ? . 129.

44. What four kinds of the *writ of habeas corpus*, are made use of by the *courts* at Westminster, for removing prisoners from one *court* to another, in the more easy administration of justice ? 129, 130.

45. What is the *habeas corpus ad respondendum?* 129.

46. What is that *ad satisfaciendum ?* 129.

47. What are those *ad prosequendum, testificandum, deliberandum,* &c. ? 129.

48. What is the common *writ ad faciendum et recipiendum;* and why is the *writ* frequently denominated an *habeas corpus cum causa?* 129, 130.

49. Upon what is this writ grantable, and what is its effect ? 130.

50. But what is ordered by the stat. 1 & 2 P. & M. c. 13. in order to prevent the surreptitious discharge of *prisoners?* 130.

51. And what is enacted by statutes 21 Jac. 1. c. 23., 12 Geo. I. c. 29., and 19 Geo. III. c. 70., in order to avoid vexatious delays, by removal of frivolous *causes ?* 130, 131.

52. But what is the great and efficacious *writ*, in all manner of illegal confinement ; what does it direct ; and when, whence, and whither does it issue ? 131, 132.

52. How must this *writ* be obtained : and why ? 132, 133.

54. When is this *writ* a *writ of right*, in whom against whom ? 133

55. What is it absolutely necessary to express upon every *commitment* ? 134.

56. What does the statute 16 Car I. c. 10. § 8. enact, as to the writ of *habeas corpus* ? 135.

57. What does the famous *habeas corpus* act, 31 Car. II. c. 2., enact ; but to what *commitments* only does it extend ? 136, 137.

58. What, if the writ be not immediately obeyed ? 137.

59. What is the *satisfactory* remedy for the *injury* of *false imprisonment ?* 138.

60. What four relations of persons do *injuries*, which affect the *relative rights* of individuals, particularly affect ? 139.

61. What are the three principal *injuries* which may be offered to a *husband ?* 139.

62. What does the law always suppose, in case of *abduction ;* and why ? 139.

63. What two species of remedy has the husband for this *injury ?* 139.

64. What satisfaction does the law give a husband for the *civil injury* of *adultery ?* 139.

64. By what circumstances are the *damages*, recovered for this *injury* increased or diminished ? 140.

66. In what cases, must *marriage* in fact be proved ? 140.

67. When does the law give the *husband* a separate remedy, by an action of trespass, *per
quod consortium amisit?*   140.

68. Of what two kinds were *injuries* that might
be offered to persons, considered in the *relations* of *parent* or *guardian ;* and, provided
either be still an *injury* what is the remedy ?   140, 141.

69. But what more speedy and summary method
of redressing all complaints, relative to *wards*
and *guardians*, hath of late obtained ; and
what is expressly provided by statute 12
Car. II. c. 24. as to *testamentary guardians ?*
141, 142.

70. What two species of *injuries* are incident to
the *relation* between *master* and *servant*, and
the rights accruing therefrom ?   142.

71. Who have what two remedies, in case one
man beat or confine another's *servant ?*   142.

CHAP. IX.

Of Injuries to Personal Property.

1. OF what two natures are the *injuries*, which
may be offered to the *rights* of *property ?*
144.

2. What are the two sorts of *injuries*, which may be offered to the rights of *personal property?* 145.

3. To what two species of *injuries*, are the *rights* of *personal property* in *possession* liable ? 145.

4. Into what two branches, is *dispossession* divisible ? 145.

5. Of what two kinds is the remedy, which the law has given for an unlawful *taking* of goods ? 145, 146.

6. By what two species of *action*, is the actual specific possession of the identical *personal chattel* restored to the proper owner ? 146.

7. Why may this be done in the case of *distress*, more than in any other ? 146.

8. What are the two species of *rescous*, and their several remedies ? 146.

9. What is an action of *replevin ;* and what do the *statutes of Marlbridge*, and of 1 P. & M. c. 12., direct the sheriff to do concerning *replevin?* 147.

10. In pursuance of the statute of Westm. 2. 13 Edw. I. c. 2., for what two things is security to be given, by the party *replevying*, to the *sheriff* or his deputy ; and what does the statute 11 Geo. II. c. 19. require besides, of the officer granting a *replevin* on a *distress* for *rent?* 147, 148.

11. But what if the *distreinor* claim any property in the goods so taken, and to keep them by a kind of *personal remitter ?* 148.

12. And what if the *sheriff* return, that the goods or beasts are *eloigned, elongata,* carried to a distance, to places to him unknown? 149.

13. When can goods taken *in withernam* be *replevied?* 149.

14. Upon *action* of *replevin* brought, when dees the *distreinor* or *defendant* make *avowry,* and when *cognizance?* 150.

15. What if the *cause* be determined for the *plaintiff*; and what, if for the *defendant*; and what does the statute of Westm. 2. c. 2. enact in this latter event? 150.

16. When shall the *plaintiff* have a *writ of second deliverance* and the *defendant* a *writ of return irreplevisable;* and what are they? 150.

17. What does the statute 17 Car. II. c. 7. direct, if the *plaintiff* in an *action* of *replevin* be *nonsuit* before *issue* joined, or if *judgment* be given against him on *demurrer;* or what, if the *nonsuit* be after *issue* joined, or if a *verdict* be against the *plaintiff?* 150, 151.

18. But what, if pending a *replevin* for a former *distress,* a man *distrein* again for the same *rent* or *service?* 151.

19. What is the remedy, if one man take the goods of another out of his possession; or what other remedy may the *party* have, at his choice, if the *taking* be without force? 151.

20. Of what two kinds, is the remedy for the un-lawful *detaining* of goods, lawfully taken ? 151, 152.

21. By what two species of *action*, may the first of these kinds of remedy be sought ? 151, 152.

22. What is necessary in an *action* of *detinue ;* and for what, therefore, cannot such *action* be brought ? 152.

23. What four points are necessary, to ground an *action* of *detinue ?* 152.

24. But what disadvantage attends this *action ;* and whence did it arise ? 152.

25. What was the *action* of *trover* and *conversion* in its original ; and why, by fiction of law, was its use enlarged to what extent ? 153.

26. What shall be recovered by an *action* of *tro-ver* and *conversion ?* 153.

27. What are the two remedies for *damage* that may be offered to *things personal*, while in the possession of the owner ? 153, 154.

28. From what do all *injuries*, affecting the *right* of *things personal*, in *action*, arise ? 154.

29. What is the twofold division of *contracts ?* 154.

30. What three distinct species do *express con-tracts* include ? 154.

31. What is the legal acceptation of *debt ?* 154.

32. What are the two species of remedy for *debt ;* and when only will the first lie ? 154, 155.

33. For what two reasons, are *actions of debt* sel-dom brought, but upon *special contracts*, under seal ?   155.

34. Wherein does an *action on the case*, or what is called an *indebitatus assumpsit*, differ from an *action of debt ?*   155, 156.

35. But what, in an *action of debt*, if the *defendant* can shew, that he has discharged any part of it ?   156.

36. When is the form of the writ of *debt*, in the *debet*, as well as the *detinet ;* and when in the *detinet* only ?   156.

37. What is a *covenant ;* and what is the remedy for a breach of one ?   156, 157.

38. What is a *covenant-real ;* and what is the remedy for a breach of one ?   157.

39. What does the statute 32 Hen. VIII. c. 34. give to the *grantee* or *assignee* of a *reversion ?* 158.

40. What is a *promise ;* and what is the remedy for a breach of one ?   158.*

---

* It may prevent the student from being misled by this part of Blackstone's Commentaries, if the compiler here transcribe part of a note, which is to be found in the first volume of Mr. Selwyn's Abridgment of the Law of Nisi Prius (2d edit. 1810, pp. 53, 54.):

" It is worthy of observation, that Sir William Blackstone, in that part of the third volume of his Commentaries wherein he treats of the action of *assumpsit*, has not either named, described, or even alluded to the consideration requisite to sup-

41. In the case of a *simple contract debt*, what is
   it that gives the *creditor* his *action on the*

---

port an *assumpsit*; and, what is more remarkable, the example
put by him, in order to illustrate the nature of the action, is,
in the terms in which it is there stated, a case of *nudum
pactum*: ' If a builder promises, undertakes, or assumes to
Caius, that he will build and cover his house within a limited
time, *and fails to do it*, Caius has an action on the case against
the builder for this breach of his express promise, undertaking, or *assumpsit*.' See 1 Roll. Abr. 9. 1. 41, Doct. and
Stud. Dial. 2. ch. 24., and Elsee *v.* Gatward, 5 T. R. 143.,
that an action will not lie for a mere nonfeasance, unless the
promise is founded on a consideration. It is possible, that the
learned Commentator might have selected his example from
Bro. Abr. tit. *Action sur le Case*, 72., without adverting to the
omission of the consideration."

However this may be, it is certainly astonishing, that the
learned Commentator should have been betrayed into this
error, with the doctrine in Roll. Abr. before him, where it is
expressly said, that "if a person promise to *build a house* for
me within a given time, no action lies for the non-performance,
unless a consideration be alleged for it," and where several
cases are cited from the Year books to support the position.
So far from the law of England acknowledging as valid any
contract founded upon no consideration, it will not even sanc-
tion a promise springing from a moral consideration; nor will
such a consideration support a legal *assumpsit*. This latter
point has been fully established by the very elaborate argu-
ment which will be found in a note to the case of Wennall
v. Adney, 3 Bos. & Pul. 247. " An express promise, there
fore, as it should seem, can only revive a precedent good consideration, which might have been enforced at law, through
the medium of an implied promise, had it not been suspended

case, instead of being driven to an *action of debt?* 159.

42. In what five cases, does the statute of frauds and perjuries, 29 Car. II. c. 3. enact, that no verbal promise shall be sufficient to ground an action upon, but at least some note or *memorandum* of it shall be made in writing, and signed by the *party,* to be charged therewith? 159.

43. From what two circumstances, do *implied contracts* arise? 159. 162.

44. What is every man bound, and hath virtually agreed, to do, by the fundamental *constitution*

---

by some positive rule of law, but can give no original right of action, if the obligation on which it is founded never could have been enforced at law, though not barred by any legal maxim or statute provision."

It may be remarked here, once for all, that the learned Commentator, throughout his book, does not take the distinction between an *action on the case* and an *action of assumpsit,* which is made by the modern pleader. " Though founded upon contract," says Mr. Chitty, in his Practical Treatise on Pleading, (vol. i. p. 88.) " this action is distinguishable from *brevia formata,* and, falling within the provision of the statute of Westminster, may be termed an *action on the case*[*]; it is now, however, uniformly called an *action of assumpsit,* and, when the term ' case' is adopted in a statute, or otherwise, an action as for a *tort,* and in form *ex delicto,* is usually intended, and not an action in form *ex contractu.* "[†]

* " Bac. Ab. *Assumpsit.* Gilb. C. P. 6. 2 Black. Rep. 850."
† " 7 T. R. 36."

of *government*, to which every man is a con-
tracting party ?   160.

45. If a *plaintiff* have once obtained a *judgment*
against a *defendant* for a certain sum, and
neglect to take out *execution* thereupon, what
action may he afterwards bring upon this
judgment, and to what proof shall he be put ?
160.

46. How does the law look upon a *forfeiture*, imposed by the *bye-laws* and private ordinances
of a *corporation*, upon any that belong to the
body, or an *amercement*, set in a *court-leet* or
court-baron, upon any of the *suitors* to the
court?   161.

47. What forfeitures do the *statute of Winchester*,
and the statute 9 Geo. I. c. 22., commonly
called the *black act*, impose upon the inha-
bitants of *hundreds?*   161.

48. What is called a *popular action*, and what a *qui
tam*; and what does the statute 4 Hen. VII.
c. 20. enact, in order to prevent the practice of
offenders, procuring their own friends to be-
gin a *qui tam action*, that may forestal and
prevent other actions ?   161.

49. What six classes of *implied contracts*, or *as-
sumpsits*, arise from the general implication
and intendment of the *courts of judicature*,
that every man hath engaged to perform what
his justice or duty requires ?   162—165.

50. What is a *writ of account, de computo* ; and against whom is it extended by statute 4 Ann. c. 16.?   164.

51. When are a *sheriff*, or *gaoler*, liable to an *action on the case* ; and when of *debt*?   165.

52. But in what case does the law imply no *general undertaking* to perform an office with integrity, diligence, and skill?   166.

53. What is an *action of deceit* (or *on the case*, in nature of a *writ of deceit*); and when may it be brought?   *165, *166.

—

CHAP. X.

Of Injuries to Real Property ; and, first, of Dispossession, or Ouster of the Freehold.

1. WHAT are the six principal *injuries* affecting *real rights*?   167.

2. What is *ouster*; and of what two kinds may it be?   167.

3. By what five methods, is *ouster* of the *freehold* effected?   167.

4. What is an *abatement*?   167, 168.

5. What is an *intrusion*; and wherein does it differ from an abatement?   169.

6. What is a *disseisin ;* and wherein does it differ from the two former species of *injury ?* 169.

7. How must *disseisin* of *things corporeal* be effected ? 170.

8. What is *disseisin* of *things incorporeal ?*   170.

9. With regard to *freehold rent* in particular, what five methods of working a *disseisin* thereof, do our antient law-books mention ?   170.

10. But when only are all these *disseisins* of *hereditaments incorporeal,* such ?   170.

11. May not something of this kind be done, even in *corporeal hereditaments,* to entitle a man to the more easy and commodious remedy of an *assise* of *novel disseisin,* instead of being driven to the more tedious process of a *writ of entry ?* 170, 171.

12. Wherein do the remaining two species of *injury,* by *ouster,* differ from the former three ? 171.

13. What is a *discontinuance ?*   171, 172.

14. What did the statute 32 Hen. VIII. c. 28, provide, as to a *discontinuance* of the *wife's* estate, by the *alienation* of the *husband ;* and what is declared by the statutes 1. Eliz. c. 19., and 13 Eliz. c. 10., as to *discontinuance* by the *alienation* of a *sole corporation ?*   172.

15. What is a *deforcement,* as contradistinguished from the former four species of *injury* by *ouster ?* 172—174.

16. What are the remedies for the several species of *injury* by *ouster?* 174.

17. What is the first method, whereby these remedies may be obtained, or that where the *tenant* or occupier of the *land* hath gained only a mere possession, and no apparent shadow of *right?* 174.

18. How must *entry* be made ; and what are making *claim*, and *continual claim?* 174, 175.

19. Upon what three only of the five species of *ouster*, does the remedy by *entry* take place.? 175.

20. What remedy has a man for *ouster* by a *tenant by sufferance?* 175, 176.

21. How may the right of *entry* be *tolled;* and why? 176, 177.

22. Yet what exceptions are there to this rule of *tolling* the right of *entry;* and how is it still farther narrowed by the statute 32 H. VIII. c. 33? 177, 178.

23. What is enacted, on the other hand, by the statute of limitations, 21 Jac. I. c. 16., and by statute 4 & 5 Ann. c. 16.? 178.

24. What is the remedy, upon an *ouster*, by the *discontinuance* of *tenant in tail*, or in case of *deforcement;* and why? 178, 179.

25. What, if one turn, or keep, another out of possession forcibly ; and what does the statute 8 Hen. VI. c. 9. enact in such case, or if any *alienation* be made to defraud the possessor of his right? 179.

26. What are the two remedies, which are in use where the *tenant* or occupier hath in him, not only a bare *possession*, but also an apparent *right* of *possession* ?   179, 180.

27. If a *recovery* be had against the *dispossessor*, in the *actions* by *writ of entry* or an *assise*, may he afterwards exert his legal claim to the *right* of ownership ?   180.

28. What is a *writ of entry* ; to whom is it directed ; and what does it require ?   180, 181.

29. Against whom must the *writ of entry* always be brought ; and what are the *degrees* called the *per*, the *per* and *cui*, and the *post*, within which *writs of entry* are brought ?   181, 182.

30. To what cases of *ouster*, is the remedy by *writ of entry* inapplicable ?   182, 183.

31. What is the origin of a *writ of assise* ; wherein does it differ from a *writ of entry* ; and can recourse be had to the one action, to set aside the decision of the other ?   184, 185.

32. To what two species of *injury* by *ouster*, is the remedy by *writ of assise* only applicable ?   185.

33. What were an *assise of mort d'ancestor*, and *writs* of *ayle*, or *de avo*, of *besayle*, or *de proavo*, of *cosinage*, or *de consanguineo*, and of *nuper obiit* ; beyond what degrees collateral and lineal was a man not allowed to have any of these actions; and why can they not now be brought ?   185—187.

34. What is an *assise* of *novel* (or recent) *disseisin;* and wherein does it differ from an *assise* of *mort d'ancestor ?*   187.

35. If the *jury* of *recogniters,* in an *assise* of *novel disseisin,* find an *actual seisin* in the *demandant,* what shall he have ?   187.

36. If a person *disseised* recover *seisin* of the *land* again, by *assises* of *novel disseisin* and *mort d'ancestor,* and be again *disseised* of the same *tenements* by the same *disseisor,* what is enacted by the statutes of *Merton, Marlberge,* and *Westm.* 2. ?   188.

37. Beyond what period does the present *statute of limitations* enact, that no person shall bring any *possessory action,* to recover possession of *lands,* and customary and prescriptive *rents, suits* and *services* merely upon the *seisin,* or dispossession of his ancestors ?   189.

38. Had it not been for the doctrine of *remitter,* how might the *tenant by remitter* have been turned out of possession ?   190.

39. What is the great and final remedy, whereby the *right of property* may be asserted, against the *right of possession ?*   191.

40. In what four cases, is this remedy, or that by such other *writs,* as are said to be of the same nature, principally applied ?   191.

41. What is the remedy, upon an *alienation* by *tenant in tail,* whereby the estate-tail is *discontinued,* and the *remainder* or *reversion* is

by failure of the *particular estate*, displaced, and turned into a mere *right ?* 191.

42. Into what three species is the writ of *formedon (secundum formam doni)* distinguished; and where does each species lie? 192.

43. What, by statute 21 Jac. I. c. 16., is the time of limitation in a *formedon ?* 192, 193.

44. What is the remedy, if the owners of a *particular estate* be *barred* of the *right of possession*, by a *recovery* had against them, through their default or non-appearance in a *possessory action ?* 193.

45. What is the remedy, in case the *right of possession* be *barred* by a *recovery* upon the merits, in a *possessory action*, or by the *statute of limitations ?* 193.

46· Of what estate only, doth a *mere writ of right* lie ; and, what, if other *actions* are, or have been, brought to recover the same estate? 193.

47. In bar of what, may a *recovery* had in this *action*, be pleaded ? 194.

48. But are there not some cases where *writs*, in the nature of *writs of right*, do not demand the *fee-simple ;* and are there not others, where the *mere writ of right*, alone is not applicable to every case of a claim of *lands* in *fee simple ?* 194, 195.

49. Where must the general *writ of right* be bo ght; and whither may it be removed ? 195.

50. What, by statute 32 Hen. VIII. c. 2., is the limitation of a *writ of right?* 196.
51. But by what *actions* is the *title* of *lands* now usually tried? 197.

———

CHAP. XI.

Of Dispossession or Ouster, of Chattels Real.

1. OF what two kinds, is *ouster* from *chattels real?* 198.
2. By what only, is *ouster* of the first kind liable to happen ; and what is the remedy for such *ouster ?* 198.
3. By what only, does *ouster* of the second kind happen ; and what two remedies has the law provided for this injury ? 199.
4. Where doth a writ of *ejectione firmæ*, or *action* of *trespass* in *ejectment* lie ; and what shall be recovered by it ? 199.
5. What is the present method, by which the remedy by *ejectment* is converted into a method of trying *titles* to the *freehold ;* who is called the *casual ejector ;* and what if the *tenant in possession* do not within a limited time apply to the *court*, to be admitted a *defendant*, in his stead ? 202, 203.
6. But, if the *tenant in possession* do apply to be made a *defendant*, upon what condition is it

allowed him; and what is the *lessor* of the *plaintiff* then bound to do ? 203, 204.

7. Yet, to prevent fraudulent recoveries of the *possession*, by collusion with the *tenant* of the *land*, what is enacted by statute of 11 Geo. II. c. 19. ? 204.

8. But what, if the new *defendants*, whether *landlord* or *tenant*, or both, after entering into the *aommon rule*, fail to appear at the *trial*, and to confess *lease*, *entry*, and *ouster?* 204, 205.

9. The *damages* recovered in these *actions* being now merely *nominal*, what *action* lies, in order to complete the remedy when the *possession* has been long detained from him that had the *right* to it ? 205.

10. Why will not a *writ of ejectment* lie, of *incorporeal hereditaments*, with what exception by the express purview of statute 32 Hen. VIII. c. 7. ? 206.

11. What does the statute 4 Geo. II. c. 28. enact as to *landlords*, whose *tenants* are in arrear ? 206.

12. Where doth the *writ* of *quare ejecit infra terminum* lie, by the antient law ; and what shall be recovered by it ? 207.

13. But why is this *action* fallen into disuse ? 207.

CHAP. XII.

Of Trespass.

1. WHAT is *trespass*, in its limited and confined sense? 209.
2. Why does the law call every *trespass* of this nature, a *breach* of another's *close?* 209, 210.
3. What is necessary, in order to be able to maintain an *action of trespass?* 210, 211.
4. In case of *trespass* by *cattle, damage feasant,* what remedy has the party injured? 211.
5. What is the *action* that lies in either of these cases of *trespass* committed upon another's land ; and when may *damages* be recovered? 211, 212.
6. What is called laying the *action* with a *continuando ;* and when only can this be done? 212.
7. In what cases is *trespass* justifiable ; but in what, shall a man be accounted a *trespasser ab initio?* 212—214.
8. What does the statute 11 Geo. II. c. 19. enact, as to *trespass* by *entry* of the *landlord* to distrem? 213.
9. What is enacted by statutes 43 Eliz. c. 6., and 22 & 23 Car. II. c. 9. § 136, in order to prevent trifling and vexatious *actions of trespass ;* but what two exceptions more have been made to this rule, by statutes 8 & 9 W. III. c. 11., and 4 & 5 W. & M. c. 23.? 214, 215.

CHAP. XIII.

Of Nusance.

1. WHAT is *nusance, nocumentum ;* and of what two kinds ? 216.
2. Of what two kinds are *private nusances,* with regard to the species of hereditaments which they may affect ? 216.
3. To what three, may the *nusances,* which affect a man's *dwelling* be reduced ? 217.
4. What are *nusances* to one's *lands ?* 217, 218.
5. What are *nusances* with regard to other *corporeal hereditaments ?* 218.
6. What are *nusances,* as to *incorporeal hereditaments ?* 218, 219.
7. What two things are necessary, in order to make out another person's setting up a *fair* or *market,* so near mine that he does me a prejudice, to be a *nusance ?* 218, 219.
8. When shall a private person have a private satisfaction, for *damage* by a *public nusance ?* 220.
9. What are the three remedies by *suit,* for a *private nusance ;* and by whom only can the last two *actions* be brought ? 220—222.
10. What, if, after one *verdict* against him, in an *action on the case* for *damages* for a *nusance,* the *defendant* continue it ? 220.

11. What is an *assise of nusance* ; and if the *assise* be found for the *plaintiff*, of what two things shall he have *judgment?*   221.
12. Does an *assise of nusance* lie against the wrong-doer who levied, or did, the *nusance,* or against the person to whom he may have aliened the *tenement,* whereon the *nusance* is situated ?   221.
13. What is a *writ quod permittat prosternere* ; and for and against whom does this *writ* extend its power ?   221, 222.
14. Why are these two last *actions* fallen into dis-use ?   222.

—

CHAP. XIV.

Of Waste.

1. WHAT is *waste, vastum* ; and of what two natures ?   223.
2. What must those persons have, who may be injured by *waste* ?   223, 224.
3. What remedy has a person, who has a *freehold right of common* of *estovers,* if the owner of the *wood* demolish the whole wood ; and what remedy has he, if he have only a *chattel-interest* in such *common* ?   224.
4. But what is the most usual and important *interest,* that is hurt by this commission of

waste ; and what remedy hath he, who hath this *interest* in case of *waste ?*   224, 225.

5. Yet why may a *parson, vicar, archdeacon, prebendary,* and the like, who are seised, in right of their churches, of any *remainder* or *reversion,* have an *action of waste ?*   225.

6. Of what two kinds is the redress for this *injury* of *waste ;* and by what process is each kind obtained ?   225.

7. What is a *writ of estrepement ;* when may it now be had ; by virtue of it, what may the *sheriff* do, if the *writ* be directed to him ; and what is the consequence of its being directed to the *tenant* himself ?   225—227.

8. Besides this preventive redress at *common law,* what will the *courts of equity* do, upon bill exhibited therein ?   227.

9. What is a *writ of waste ;* and by, and against, whom, may it be brought ?   227.

10. Why is this *action* also maintainable, in pursuance of the statute Westm. 2., by one *tenant in common* or *joint tenant* of the *inheritance,* against another, who makes *waste* in the *estate* holden in *common* or *joint tenancy,* but not by one *coparcener* against another ?   227.

11. Wherein is the *action of waste* a *real action ;* and what shall be recovered, if the *waste* be proved ?   228.

12. What, if the *defendant* in the *action* make default in *appearance* to the *writ;* and what, if he suffer *judgment* to go against him by default, or upon a *nihil dicit?* 228.

———

CHAP. XV.

Of Subtraction.

1. WHAT is *subtraction;* and wherein does it differ from *disseisin?* 230.
2. Of what two kinds, are the *rents* or other *services*, the *subtraction* of which varies the remedy in the same degree? 230.
3. What are *duties* and *services*, usually issuing and arising *ratione tenuræ;* and what is the general remedy for their *subtraction?* 231.
4. What is called a *distress infinite;* and when may it be taken? 231.
5. What five other remedies for *subtraction* of *rents* or *services* are there? 231—233.
6. What is the effect of the *writ de consuetudinibus et servitiis?* 232.
7. What is the *writ of cessavit*: and when, by the statute of Glocester, does it not lie? 232, 233.
8. What is a *writ of right, sur disclaimer?* 233, 234.

9. But what two *writs* has the law given the *tenant*, to remedy the oppression of the *lord?*   234.

10. What is the *writ ne injuste vexes;* and where does it lie ?   234.

11. What is *writ of mesne de medio;* and where does it lie ?   234.

12. What are *services,* due by antient *custom* and *prescription;* and what are the remedies for their *subtraction ?*   235.

———

CHAP. XVI.

Of Disturbance.

1. WHAT is *disturbance;* and of what five sorts ? 236.

2. When does *disturbance* of *franchises* happen ; and what are its remedies ? 236, 237.

3. What are the three species of *disturbance* of *common?*   237, 240.

4. When does the first species of *disturbance* of *common* happen ; and what are its remedies ? 237.

5. What is *surcharging* a *common;* and when can it happen?   237, 238.

6. What are the usual remedies for *surcharging* a *common;* 238.

7. What is a *writ of admeasurement of pasture;* where does it lie ; who is entitled to it ; to

whom is it directed ; and how must it be executed ?   238, 239.

8. What, if after the *admeasurement* have ascertained the *right*, the same *defendant surchar-
ges* the *common* again ?   239.

9. What is *disturbance* of *common*, by enclosure, or
obstruction ; and what are its remedies ?   240.

10. But are there not cases, in which the *lord* may
enclose and abridge the *common* ?   240, 241.

11. When does *disturbance* of *ways* happen ; how
is this species of *injury* distinguished from
that of *nusance* ; and what is the remedy for
it ?   241. 242.

12. What is *disturbance* of *tenure* ; and who has
what remedy for it ?   242.

13. What is *disturbance* of *patronage*; and how
was it distinguished at *common law* from
another species of *injury*, called *usurpation* ?
242, 243.

14. How is the title of *usurpation* now narrowed ; and upon what foundation stands the law
of it ?   244.

15. What three persons may be *disturbers* of a
right of advowson ; and to whom has the law
given what three remedies for the *disturbance* ?   245.

16. When does an assise of *darrein presentment*,
or *last presentation*, lie ; but why is it fallen
into disuse ?   245, 246.

17. What is a *jus patronatus* ; and when must it
be awarded ?   246, 247.

18. What is a *duplex querela;* and when may it be had? 247.

19. What is a *writ* of *quare impedit;* why, in the case of another *presentation* being set up, is it most advisable, to bring it against the *bishop*, the *patron*, and the *clerk* too; and what does the *writ* command? 247, 248.

20. What is a *writ* of *ne admittas;* when may it be had; and what, if the *bishop*, after the receipt of it, admit any person? 248.

21. In the proceedings upon a *quare impedit*, what must the *plaintiff* prove; and, upon failure of the *plaintiff's* proof, what must the *defendant?* 249.

22. But if the *right* be found for the *plaintiff*, what three farther points are also to be inquired? 249.

23. If it be found that the *plaintiff* hath the right, and hath commenced his *action* in due time, then what *judgment* shall he have? 249, 250.

24. But what, if the *church* remain still void, at the end of the *suit?* 250.

25. And what, if the *bishop* do not admit the *clerk* upon this? 250.

26. What is the advantage of a *writ of right of advowson* over a *writ* of *quare impedit?* 250.

27. Why is there no limitation, with regard to the time, within which any *actions* touching *advowsons,* are to be brought? 250, 251.

23

28. But is there not one species of *presentation* in which, by virtue of several *acts of parliament,* a remedy, to be sued for in the *temporal courts,* is put into the hands of the *clerks* presented, as well as of the owners of the *advowson;* and with what powers particularly are the *patrons* clothed by the statutes of 12 Ann. st. 2. c. 14. § 4., and 11 Geo. II. c. 17. ? 251, 252.

29. But when the *clerk* is in full possession of the *benefice,* what possessory remedies does the law give him ; and when is he entitled to a special remedy, called a *writ* of *juris utrum,* or the *parsons writ* of *right;* but why is this remedy now of very little use ?   252, 253.

CHAP. XVII.

Of Injuries proceeding from, or affecting the Crown.

1. OF what two natures are *injuries,* to which the *crown* is a *party ?*   254.

2. What are the two *common-law* methods of obtaining possession, or restitution from the *crown,* of either *real* or *personal property;* and when may each be resorted to ?   256, 257.

3. What are the six methods of redressing such *injuries* as the *crown* may receive from the *subject ?*   257, 258. 260—262. 264.

4. Whar *actions* cannot the *King* maintain ? 257.

5. What is an *inquisition*, or *inquest of office* ? 258—260.

6. What remedy may the *subject* have, in order to avoid the possession of the *crown*, acquired by the *finding* of such *office*, besides his *petition of right*, and his *monstrans de droit* ? 260.

7. By whom may a *writ* of *scire facias* to repeal the *King's patent* or *grant* be brought ? 260, 261.

8. What is an *information* on behalf of the *crown*, filed in the *exchequer*; and of what two sorts are the most usual *informations* ? 261.

9. What is an *information in rem* ? 262.

10. When does a *writ* of *quo warranto* lie in the *King*; and why has it given way to an *information* in the nature of such a *writ* ? 262, 263.

11. To what is this proceeding now applied, by virtue of the statute 9 Ann. c. 20. ? 264.

12. For what is the *writ* of *mandamus* made a most full and effectual remedy by the same statute, and by statute 11 Geo. I. c. 4.; what are the proceedings on this *writ*; and what is a *writ of restitution* ? 264, 265.

CHAP. XVIII.

*Of the Pursuit of Remedies by Action; and, first, of
the Original Writ.*

1. WHAT are the eight general and orderly parts
of a *suit* in the *court of common pleas?* 272.
2. What is an *original,* or *original writ;* where is
it sued out; and what and where is its *return?* 273.
3. What is the foundation of suits, below the value
of forty shillings? 273.
4. Of what two sorts are *original writs;* and
where is each sort in use? 274.
5. What is the security given by the *plaintiff* for
prosecuting his claim? 274, 275.
6. What and when, is the *return* of each sort of
writ? 275.
7. What is the origin of the *terms;* and what are
they? 275—277.
8. What are *days in bank, dies in banco?* 277.
9. What is called the *essoign day* of the *term?*
277, 278.
10. What is the *quarto die post?* 278.

CHAP. XIX,

Of Process.

1. WHAT is the *process ;* and, to distinguish it from what two other kinds, is it called *original process ?* 279.
2. Of what nine sorts, is *original process ?* 279—284. 287, 288. 290, 291.
3. What is the *summons;* and how is it made? 279, 280.
4. What is the *writ of attachment* or *pone ;* and when is this the first and immediate *process?* 280.
5. What is the *writ* of *distringas*, or *distress infinite ?* 280.
6. What is the *writ* of *capias ad respondendum ;* and, upon what species of complaint may it now be had, by several statutes ? 281, 282.
7. For what reason, does the practice of commencing almost all *actions*, by bringing an *original writ* of *trespass, quare clausum fregit, vi et armis*, still continue ? 281, 282.
8. Why are *writs*, subsequent to the *original writ*, called *judicial writs ?* 282.
9. Is this regular and orderly method of *process* now gone through ; or, what is now usual in practice ? 282.

10. When does a writ *testatum capias* issue ; and what, if the *action* be brought in one *county*, and the *defendant* live in another ?   283.

11. But what, if a *defendant* abscond, and the *plaintiff* would proceed to an *outlawry* against him ?   283.

12. What are *alias* and *pluries writs*, and *writs of exigent*, or *exigi facias*, and *proclamation* ? 283, 284.

13. What is the effect of *outlawry;* what is the *writ* of *capias utlegatum* ; and how may *outlawry* be reversed ?   284.

14. What is the usual method of proceeding in the *court of King's bench?*   285.

15. What is the origin of the *process of bill of Middlesex ;* why is it so called ; and what is it ? 285.

16. When does a *writ of latitat* issue ; and when may the *bill of Middlesex*, in the *court of King's bench*, be treated like the *capias ad respondendum* in the *court of common pleas ?*   286.

17. What is the first *process* in the *court of exchequer ;* and what does it allege ?   286.

18. What is now become the effect of the *capias, latitat*, &c. ; what, if the *defendant* appear upon them ; and what, if he do not ?   287.

19. But what, if the *plaintiff* will make *affidavit*, that the cause of *action* amounts to ten pounds or upwards ; and what is required by statute 13 Car. II. st. 2. c. 2. ?   287.

20. What is the origin of the clause of *ac etiam* in a *bill of Middlesex*, and *writ of capias*; and what is it? 288.

21. When, in an *arrest*, may the *bailiff* justify breaking open the house in which the *defendant* is, in order to take him? 288.

22. Who are constantly privileged from *arrests*, and from *outlawries*; and how must an *appearance* be enforced against such persons? 288, 289.

23. Who are *pro tempore* privileged from *arrests*; and where can no *arrest* be made? 289.

24. What is the *King's writ of protection*; and what is enacted by the statute 25 Edw. III. st. 5. c. 19. as to the power of another *creditor* to proceed against a *debtor* of the *King*? 289, 290.

25. When may an *arrest* be made, or *process* served, upon a *Sunday*? 290.

26. What is *special bail* to the *sheriff*, or *bail below*; and what, if the *sheriff* do not keep the *defendant*, so as to be forthcoming in *court*? 290.

27. For what sum shall the *sheriff* take *bail*, by statute 12 Geo. I. c. 29.? 290.

28. What is *bail to the action*, or *above*; and what may the *plaintiff* require of the *sheriff*, if this be not put in? 290, 291.

29. Before whom must the *bail above* enter into what *recognizance*; and what, if they be excepted to? 291

———

CHAP. XX.

Of Pleading.

6. What was antiently understood by the word *suit?* 295.

7. When is a *nonsuit* or *non prosequitur* entered; and to what is that *plaintiff* liable, who is *non pros'd?* 295, 296.

8. What is a *retraxit*; and how does it differ from a *nonsuit?* 296.

9. What is a *discontinuance;* and what does the statute 1 Edw. VI. c. 7. enact, as to *discontinuance?* 296.

10. What is a *defence,* in its true legal sense? 296, 297.

11. What is *cognizance of the suit;* and when must it be claimed? 298.

12. What is an *imparlance;* and when is the *defendant* entitled to how many *imparlances?* 299.

13. What is a *view;* and when may it be demanded? 299.

14. What is *oyer;* and of what may it be craved? 299.

15. What is *praying in aid;* what is *voucher,* and when is it not allowed; and what is a *writ of warrantia chartæ?* 299, 300.

16. What is *praying age;* and when shall it not be had? 300, 301.

17. Of what two sorts are *pleas;* and when cannot *pleas* of the former sort be pleaded? 301.

18. Of what three kinds are *dilatory pleas?* 301, 302.

19. What effect upon a *suit* hath the death of one of the *parties;* and when can it be revived, either by or against the *executors* or other *representatives* of the deceased *party?* 302.

20. What, by the statute 4 & 5 Ann. c. 16., is essential to the admission of a *dilatory plea;* what is a rule as to the admission of *exceptions* against a *declaration* or *writ;* and in what suit shall no abatement take place, by statute 8 & 9 W. III. c. 31. ? 302.

21. To what three things does each of these kinds of *dilatory pleas* conclude ? 303.

22. What if these *dilatory pleas* be *allowed;* and what, if they be *overruled?* 303.

23. In what two ways, is a *plea to the action* made ? 303.

24. In what instance is *confession* of the whole *complaint* made in a *plea to the action ?* 303.

25. What is the effect of a *plea of tender* by the *debtor,* and *refusal* by the *creditor?* 303.

26. In what two instances, is one part of the *complaint confessed,* and the rest *traversed* or *denied ?* 304.

27. What is the effect of *paying money into court ;* and upon what may it be done ? 304.

28. What is a *motion ?* 304.

29. Of what two kinds are *pleas,* that totally *deny* the cause of *complaint ?* 305.

30. What is the *general issue,* or *general plea ?* 305.

either side traverses or denies the facts *plead-ed* by his antagonist ?   313.

43. But what, if either *side plead* a *special* nega-tive *plea*, not traversing or denying any thing that was before alleged, but disclosing some new negative matter ?   313.

—————

CHAP. XXI.

Of Issue and Demurrer.

1. WHAT is *issue exitus;* and upon what two matters ?   314.

2. What is an *issue* upon matter of *law* called ?   314.

3. What is a *demurrer ;* and, in case of exceptions to the form or manner of *pleading*, what must the *party demurring* do, by statutes 27 Eliz. c. 5., and 4 & 5 Ann. c. 16. ?   314, 315.

4. Upon either a *general* or a *special demurrer*, what must the opposite *party* do, in order to put the *parties* at *issue* in point of *law ;* and who must determine that *issue?*   315.

5. What is an *issue* of *fact ;* when is it *joined ;* and what is the principal method, by which it must be determined ?   315.

6. What is *continuance :* what, if the omission be on the part of the *plaintiff* ; and what, if it be on the part of the *defendant?*   316.

7. What is a *plea puis darrein continuance* ; what is its effect ; and when is it not allowed to be put in ? 316, 317.

8. What are *paper-books* ; and what is the *record ?* 317.

———

CHAP. XXII.

Of the several Species of Trial.

1. WHAT is *trial;* and what are the seven species of *trial* in civil cases ? 330.

2. In what particular instance, is *trial* by *record* used ; what is it ; and what may it *try ?* 330, 331.

3. What is *trial* by *inspection* or *examination ;* and when shall it be had ? 331—333.

4. What is *trial* by *certificate ;* and in what six cases shall it be had recourse to ? 333— 336.

5. What is *trial* by *witnesses, per testes ;* and when only is it allowed in *our* law ? 336.

6. What is *trial* by *wager of battel, vadiato duelli ;* in what cases was it used ; what is the form of it ; and by what has it been superseded ? 337—341.

7. What is *trial* by *wager of law, vadiatio legis ;* what is the manner of *waging law ;* in what

actions only is the *defendant* admitted to *wage his law;* who shall not be permitted to *wage law;* and how has the species of *trial* become obsolete ?   341—348.

CHAP. XXIII.

Of Trial by Jury.

1. OF what antiquity is *trial by jury*, called also *trial per pais* or *by the country;* and what does *magna carta* declare concerning it ? 349, 350.

2. Of what two kinds are *trials* by *jury*, in civil causes ?   351.

3. What is the first species of *extraordinary trial* by *jury?*   351.

4. What is another species of *extraordinary jury* ? 351.

5. What are the eight *processes* of the *ordinary trial* by *jury* ?   352. 356—358. 364, 365. 367. 375.

6. What is the writ of *venire facias;* and when and where must the *sheriff* return it, by virtue of the statute 42 Edw. III. c. 11. ?   352, 353.

7. What are called *issuable terms*, and why; and what is the *sheriff's panel?*   353.

8. What, in the *common pleas*, is called a *writ of habeas corpora juratorum*, and, in the *king's*

bench, a *distringas ;* and what is the *entry* on the *roll,* or *record ?*   354.

9. What, if the *sheriff* be not an indifferent person ; and who are called *elisors,* or *electors ?* 354, 355.

10. What, if, on the general day of trials, the *plaintiff* do not *enter* the record ?   356.

11. What is called the *trial* by *proviso ;* but why hath this practice begun to be disused, since the statute 14 Geo. II. c. 17. ?   356, 357.

12. In case the *plaintiff* intend to try the cause, what *notice* of *trial* is he bound to give the *defendant ;* and what, if the *plaintiff* then change his mind, and do not countermand the *notice* how many days before the trial ? 357.

18. How may the *trial* be deferred, however, by either *party ?*   357.

14. To whom does the *sheriff* return his *writ* of *habeas corpora,* or *distringas,* with what annexed ?   357.

15. Of what two sorts are *jurors ?*   357.

16. What is the *sheriff's* duty, upon *motion* in *court,* and a *rule* granted thereupon, for a *special jury ;* and how, and by whom, is it *struck ?*   357, 358.

17. By the statute 3 Geo. II. c. 25., who is entitled to have a *special jury* struck, upon what *trial ;* and, by statute 24 Geo II. c. 18., when shall the expence of a *special jury* not fall upon the party requiring it ?   358.

18. What is a *common jury;* and what are the directions of the statute 3 Geo. II. c. 25., concerning it ?   358.

19. What is a *view;* and how, and by whom, shall it be appointed ?   358.

20. Of what two sorts, are *challenges* of *jurors ?* 358.

21. What are *challenges* to the *array;* and upon what accounts may they be made?   359. 360.

22. Where one *party* to the *suit* is an *alien,* of whom shall the *jury* consist; but what, if both *parties* be *aliens?*   360.

23 What are *challenges* to the *polls, in capita;* and to what four heads are they reduced by Sir Edward Coke ?   361.

24. Can *judges* and *justices* be *challenged ?*   361.

25. What is a *writ de ventre inspiciendo ?*   362.

26. What, by a variety of statutes, is a *disqualification* for *juror* in point of *estate* ; but what when the *jury* is *de medietate linguæ ?*   362. 363.

27. Of what two sorts, is a *challenge propter affectum,* for suspicion of bias or partiality ; what, if the causes of *challenge* of the first sort be true ; and to whom is it given to try the validity of *challenges* of the second sort ?   363.

28. With regard to what causes of *challenge,* may a *juror* himself be examined on oath of *voir dire, veritatem dicere ?*   364.

29. Who are *excused* from serving on *juries ?* 364.

30. Who may pray a *tales,* and what is it ; and for this purpose, when must a *writ* of *decem tales, octo tales,* and the like still be issued to the *sheriff;* but by virtue of the statute 35 Hen. VIII. c. 16. when may the *judge* award a *tales de circumstantibus,* and what is it ? 364, 365.

31. To what are the *jurors* sworn ? 365.

32. What is the course of proceeding upon the trial ? 366, 367.

33. What is the definition of *evidence ?* 367.

34. Of what two kinds is *evidence* in the *trial* by *jury?* 367.

35. Of what sorts are *proofs ?* 367.

36. What two written *proofs* or *evidence* prove themselves : and what are the other two, and how must they be verified ? 367, 368.

37. What is one general rule of *evidence* that runs through all the doctrine of *trials ;* and upon what principle is *hearsay evidence* in general not admitted ? 368.

38. To what transactions does the statute 7 Jac. I. c. 12. confine the admission of *books of account* to be read in *evidence,* if the servant who was accustomed to make the *entries* in it be dead, and his *hand-writing* proved? 368, 369.

39. What is the *writ* of *subpœna ad testificandum ;* but when is no *witness* bound to appear, or to give *evidence ?* 369.

40. Who are competent *witnesses?* 369, 370.

41. How many *witnesses* are sufficient *evidence* of any single fact? 370

42 When is *positive proof* required; and when is *circumstantial* or *presumptive, evidence* admitted? 371.

43. What weight have severally, *violent presumption, probable presumption* and *light presumption?* 371.

44. Need the *witness* tell all he knows of the matter in question, whether interrogated to every point or not? 372.

45. What if the *judge,* either in his directions or decisions, mis-state the *laws* by ignorance, inadvertence or design? 372.

46. What is a *demurrer* to *evidence;* and by whom shall it be determined? 372.

47. But what practice has greatly superseded the recourse to either of these last *proceedings?* 373.

48. What are the advantages of *testimony ore tenus?* 373.

49. What is the modern doctrine as to such *evidence* as the *jury* may have, in their own consciences, by their private knowledge of facts? 374, 375.

50. What is the *summing up* of the *evidence* by the *judge?* 375.

51. How is the delivery of the *jury's verdict, veredictum,* accelerated; and what, if the *jurors*

eat or drink at all, or have any eatables about them, without consent of the *court*? 375.

52. What circumstances will set aside the *verdict*? 375, 376.

53. What, if the *plaintiff* do not appear to the *verdict*? 376.

54. What is the form of a voluntary *nonsuit*; and why is it more eligible for the *plaintiff* than a *verdict* against him? 376, 377.

55. Of what two kinds is a *verdict*; and when is a *verdict* of the first kind of no force? 377.

56. What have the *jury* also to do, if they *find issue* for the *plaintiff*? 377.

57. What is a *special verdict*; and by whom is it afterwards determined? 377.

58. What is another method of *finding* a species of *special verdict*; and what advantage has this over the other kind of *special verdict*? 378.

59. In both these cases, *must* the *jury* return a *special verdict*; and are they incompetent to decide the complicated question of *fact* and *law*? 378.

60. What are the four principal defects, incident to a *trial* by *jury*? 382, 383.

61. What is a *subpœna duces tecum*? 382.

CHAP. XXIV.

Of Judgment and its Incidents.

1. WHAT is a *postea?*   386.
2. What is *judgment* ; and till when, and till what can it not be *entered?*   386. 387.
3. What are causes of *suspending* the *judgment,* by granting a *new trial?*   387.
4. What if two *juries* agree in the same, or a similar *verdict?*   387.
5. What is a *new trial;* upon what proceedings is it granted; and where is it not granted?   391, 392.
6. How has the *court,* in granting a *new trial.* an opportunity of supplying the defects in the *trial* by jury ; and within what time must the *motion* for a *new trial* be made?   392.
7. From what causes, do *arrests* of *judgment* arise?   393.
8. What is an invariable rule with regard to *arrests* of *judgment* upon matter of *law;* and will this rule hold *e converso?*   394.
9. What is a *repleader quod partes replacitent;* and when will the *court* award it?   395.
10. What is *judgment;* and of what four sorts?   395, 396.
11. Whose determination and sentence is the *judgment;* and what words constitute the *style* of the *judgment?*   396.

12. Of what two natures, are all these four species of *judgments?* 396.
13. What is judgment of *respondeat ouster?* 396, 397.
14. What are the *interlocutory judgments* most usually spoken of; when only can they happen; when are they absolutely complete; and when, and for what purpose, must a *jury* be called in? 397, 398.
15. What is a *warrant of attorney to confess a judgment;* and what does the statute 4&5 W.&M. c. 20. require, in order to its validity? 397, 398,
16. What is a *writ of inquiry* to *assess damages?* 398.
17. What are *final judgments;* and is the *party,* against whom *judgment* is given, liable to any *fine* to the *king,* or *imprisonment* till that *fine* be paid? 398, 399.
18. Which *party* shall pay the *costs* of the *suit?* 399, 400.
19. Who are not liable to pay *costs?* 400.
20. What is enacted by statutes 43 Eliz. c. 6., 21 Jac. I. c. 16., and 22 & 23 Car. II. c. 9. § 136., to prevent trifling and malicious *actions,* for *words,* for *assault and battery,* and for *trespass,* with what two exceptions, by statutes 4 & 5 W. & M. c. 23., and 8 & 9 W. III. c. 11? 401.
21. What follows after *judgment,* unless what? 401.

CHAP. XXV.

Of Proceedings in the Nature of Appeals.

1. OF what four principal kinds are *proceedings*, in the nature of *appeals* from the *proceedings* of the *king's court of law?* 402. 405, 406.

2. What is a *writ of attaint;* when at *common law*, must it be brought ; and on what *issue* only does it not lie ? 402—404.

3. What *jury* are to *try* this *false verdict;* what are the qualifications of the *jurors* by statute 15 Hen. VI. c. 5. ; and which party only is allowed to produce new matter, and why ? 404.

4. What was the *judgment* by the common law, if the *grand jury found the verdict* a *false* one? 404.

5. But what was enacted by several statutes, as to the time when an *attaint* may be brought, and as to the punishment of the *attainted jurors?* 405.

6. But what has superseded the use of *attaints?* 405.

7. What is the *writ of deceit?* 405.

8. What is an *audita querela ;* and for what two persons does it lie ? 405, 406.

9. But what has rendered this *writ* almost useless ? 406.

10. But what is the principal method of redress for erroneous *judgments* in the king's *courts of record?* 406

11. What is the *writ*, to amend errors in a *base court*, not of *record?* 407.

12. Upon what matter only, does a *writ of error* lie? 407.

13. Till when, may the *record* be amended ; and what is the effect of the statutes of *amendment* and *jeofails?* 407, 408.

14. What is required of him that brings the *writ*, if it be brought to reverse any *judgment* of an *inferior court of record*, where the damages are less than ten pounds, or if it be brought to reverse the *judgment* of any *superior court* after *verdict?* 410*.

15. From what *courts*, lies the *writ of error* into the *king's bench?* 410*.

16. Whence lies the *writ of error* into the *court of exchequer-chamber;* and before whom ? 410*.

17. Whence lies the *writ of error* into the *house of peers?* and thence whence? 410*, 411*.

CHAP. XXVI.

Of Execution.

1. WHAT is *execution ;* and how is it performed ? 412.

1. What are *writs* of *habere facias seisinam* and *habere facias possessionem*; to whom are they directed; what is justifiable in their *execution*; and what is sufficient *execution*?   412.

3. What is a *writ de clerico admittendo*; and to whom is it directed?   412.

4. When does a special *writ* of *execution* issue to the *sheriff*?   412, 413.

5. What *writ* shall the *plaintiff* have, where one part of the *judgment* is *quod nocumentum amoveatur*? what is the *writ of execution* upon a *replevin*; what shall the *defendant* have, if the *distress* be *eloigned*; and what shall the *plaintiff* have, after *judgment* in *detinue*? 413.

6. Of what five sorts are *executions* in *actions*, where *money* only is recovered, as a *debt* or *damages*, and not any specific *chattel*?   413.

7. What is the *writ* of *capias ad satisfaciendum*; and against whom does it not lie?   414, 415.

8. To whom shall the *capias* issue, if an *action* be brought against a *husband* and *wife*, for the *debt* of the *wife*, when sole; and to whom, if the *action* were brought against her before her *marriage*?   414.

9. What, if *judgment* be recovered against a *husband* and *wife*, for the contract, or personal misbehaviour, of the *wife*, during her *coverture*?   411.

10. What exemption has the man, who is taken in *execution* upon this *writ*; and what does the

statute 21. Jac. 1. c. 24. enact, if the *defendant* die, while charged in *execution* upon this *writ?*   414.

11. What *executory process* may be sued out for *costs?*   415.

12. What, if after a *defendant* is once in custody upon this *process*, he be seen at large ?   415.

13. Of what two natures are *escapes;* and when shall the *sheriff* answer for the debt ?   415.

14. Will a *rescue* of a *prisoner* in *execution* excuse the *sheriff?*   415.

15. But what does the statute 32 Geo. II. c. 28. enact, in favor of *defendants*, charged in *execution?*   415, 416.

16. Yet what powers have *creditors* over their *debtors* on the other hand ?   416.

17. In what case, may the *plaintiff* set out a writ of *scire facias* against the *bail ;* and what is its effect ?   416, 417.

18. What is a *writ* of *fieri facias ;* against whom does it lie ; what doors may be broken open in its *execution ;* who must be first paid to what amount ; and what further remedy has the *plaintiff*, if part only of the *debt* be *levied* on a *fieri facias ?*   417.

19. What is a *writ* of *levari facias ;* and by what is its use superseded ?   417.

20. What is a *writ* in the nature of a *levari* or *fieri facias*, to levy the *debt* and *damage de*

26

bonis ecclesiasticis; to whom is it directed ; and by what is it followed ?　418.

21. What is the *writ* of *eligit;* what *lands* are not liable to be taken in *execution* upon a *judgment;* what, in case of a debt to the *King,* by *magna carta,* c. 8., and in what case only, can a *capias ad satisfaciendum* be had after an *eligit?*　418, 419.

22. What is an *extent* or *extendi facias;* and upon what *prosecutions* may it be had ?　419, 420.

23. What by statute 33 Hen. VIII. c. 39. of all *obligations* made to the *King;* and what *lands* of a *debtor* does the *King's judgment,* or that of any of his *officers* mentioned in the statute 13 Eliz. c. 4., affect more than the *subject's?* 420.

24. By the *statute of frauds,* 29 Car. II. c. 3., from what day shall the *judgment* bind the *land* in the hands of a *bonâ fide* purchaser; and from what day, shall the *writ* of *execution* bind the *goods* in the hands of a stranger or purchaser ?　421.

25. When the *plaintiff's* demand is satisfied, what ought to be entered on the *record?*　421.

26. But within what time must all these *writs* be sued out ?　421.

27. Yet, if this had not been the case, what will the *court* grant, in pursuance of statute Westm. 2. 13 Edw. I. c. 45.; or what other remedy has the *plaintiff?*　421, 422.

CHAP. XXVII.

Of Proceedings in the Courts of Equity.

1. WHAT four matters of *equity* are peculiar to the jurisdiction of the *court of chancery?* 426—428.

2. When has the *court of chancery* a right to appoint a *guardian;* and whither lies the *appeal* in all proceedings relative thereto ? 427.

3. How only can the proceedings, to enquire whether or no the *party* be an *idiot* or *lunatic,* be redressed, if erroneous ? 427.

4. On the other hand, doth not the jurisdiction of the *court of chancery* fail to extend to some *causes,* wherein relief may be had in the *court of exchequer,* and the *duchy court of Lancaster ?* 428, 429.

5. What is *equity* in its true and genuine meaning; and does *equity* differ from *law ?* 429—436.

6. What are the five essential differences, whereby the *courts of equity* are distinguished from the *courts of law ?* 436.

7. What does a *court of equity,* in the way of *proof,* when facts, or their leading circumstances, rest only in the knowledge of the *party;* and, for want of this discovery at law, in what matters have the *courts of equity* acquired a concurrent jurisdiction with every other *court ?* 437, 438.

8. What authority and jurisdiction have courts of equity in *interrogatories* administered to *witnesses*; and in what cases, on this account, do they exercise the same jurisdiction, which might have been exercised at law? 438.

9. In what cases does the want of a more specific remedy, than can be obtained in the *courts of law*, give a concurrent jurisdiction to a *court of equity?* 438, 439.

10. What are the fifteen *proceedings* in the *courts of equity?* 442—445.

11. What is a *bill*; what does it always pray; and when does it pray also an *injunction?* 442.

12. What if the *bill* do not call all necessary *parties*, however remotely interested, before the *court*; by whom must it be signed; and what, if it contain matter either scandalous or impertinent? 442, 443.

13. Where must the *bill* be filed; and when will the *court* grant an *injunction* immediately? 443

14. What is the *process* of *subpœna*; and, what if the *defendant* do not appear within the time limited by the rules of the *court*, and *plead, demur,* or *answer* to the *bill?* 443.

15. What are the respective *processes* of *contempt*, in their successive order; what, if the *defendant* abscond; and what, if he be taken? 444, 445.

16. What is the *process* against a *corporate body*; what against a *peer*; and what against a *member* of the *house of commons?*   445.

17. What does the statute 5 Geo. II. c. 25. enact, where the *defendant* cannot be found to be served with *process* of *subpœna?*   445.

18. What is a *demurrer* in *equity?*   446.

19. Of what three kinds are *pleas*; and may a *defendant plead*, *demur*, and *answer* too?   446.

20. Why are *exceptions* to *formal minutiæ* in the *pleadings* in *equity* not allowed?   446.

21. What is an answer; when is it given upon *oath*, and when not; and when upon *honour?*   446.

22. Before whom must the *defendant* be sworn to his *answer*; by whom must the *answer* be signed; and when may it be excepted to for insufficiency?   447, 448.

23. If the *defendant* have any relief to pray against the *plaintiff*, how must it be done?   448.

24. When may the *plaintiff* amend his *bill*; and when must he have recourse to a *supplemental bill?*   448.

25. What is a *bill* of *revivor*; and what a *bill* of *inter-pleader*; and what must be annexed to this last *bill?*   448.

26. What, if the *plaintiff* chuse to proceed to the *hearing* of the *cause*, upon *bill* and *answer* only?   448.

27. What is a *replication ;* and how does the *defendant* join *issue ?*   448, 449.

28. How, and by whom, are *witnesses* examined ; of what nature must the *interrogatories* be ; to what are *examiners* and their *clerks* sworn ; and how are they compellable to appear and submit to *examination ?*   449.

29. What is a *bill to perpetuate the testimony of witnesses ?*   450.

30. When may a *rule to pass publication of witnesses* be had ?   450.

31. By whom, and before whom, may the *cause* be set down for a *hearing ?*   450.

32. What, if the *plaintiff* do not attend, upon *subpœna* to hear *judgment ;* and what, if the *defendant ?*   451.

33. When may a *plaintiff's bill* be dismissed for want of *prosecution ?*   451.

34. What is the method of hearing *causes* in *court ?*   451.

35. Of what two natures, is the *chancellor's decree ?*   452.

36. When does the *court of chancery* direct a *feigned issue* to be tried at the bar of the *court of King's bench,* or at the *assises ;* and what is the *fiction ?*   452.

37. What does the *court* refer to the opinion of the *courts of King's bench* or *common pleas,* upon a *case stated ;* and what is done there in consequence ?   452, 453.

THE END OF THE THIRD BOOK.

BOOK THE FOURTH.

OF PUBLIC WRONGS.

———

CHAPTER I.

Of the Nature of Crimes, and their Punishment.

1. WHAT are the six considerations, in treating of *public wrongs*, or *crimes* and *misdemesnors* ? 1, 2.
2. Why is the code of criminal law, with us in England, denominated the doctrine of the *pleas of the crown* ? 2.
3. From what circumstances, have the defects and disproportions in our criminal code arisen ? 3, 4.
4. What is a *crime* or *misdemesnor* ; and how has common usage distinguished the one from the other ? 5.
5. In what does the distinction of *public wrongs* from *private*, of *crimes* and *misdemesnors* from *civil injuries*, principally consist ? 5.
6. Which includes the other ? 6.

7. In what *crimes*, why cannot satisfaction be made, both to the individual and the community ; and in what, how may it ?   6, 7.

8. What double view, then, has the law, in taking cognizance of all *wrongs* or unlawful acts ? 7.

9. What are *punishments ?*   7.

10. In whom was the right of punishing *crimes* against the *law of nature* vested by that law ? 7, 8.

11. What right has the temporal legislator to inflict discretionary penalties for *crimes* against the *law of nature*, or *mala in se ?*   7, 8.

12. What right has he to inflict *punishment* for *offences* against the laws of society, or *mala prohibita ?*   8.

13. When only is a legislature warranted in inflicting the *punishment* of *death* for *offences* of human institution ?   9, 10.

14. Is it found by experience, that *capital punishments* are more effectual in preventing *crimes*, than lighter penalties ?   10.

15. What is the *end*, or final cause of human *punishment ?*   11.

16. In what three ways, is the *end* of human *punishment* effected ?   11, 12.

17. By what must the *measure* of human *punishment* be determined ?   12.

18. Why is not the *lex talionis*, or law of retaliation, in all cases, an adequate or permanent rule of *punishment ?*   12, 13.

27

19. Does the punishment of *death* with *death*, proceed upon the principle of retaliation ? 13, 14.

20. In what class of *crimes*, is the *lex talionis* more proper to be inflicted, than in any other ; and, upon this principle, what was enacted by statute 17 Edw. III. c. 18., and how long was this the law ? 14.

21. What are some general principles, drawn from the nature and circumstances of the *crime*, that may be of some assistance in allotting it an adequate *punishment ?* 15, 16, 17.

22. Why is *treason* in conspiring the *King's death* punished with greater rigour than even actually killing any private *subject ?* 15.

23. Why, generally, is a design to transgress not so flagrant an enormity, as the actual completion of that design ; and why then in the case of a treasonable conspiracy, will the bare intention to kill the *King* deserve the highest degree of severity ? 15.

24. Why is it, in more cases, *capital* for a *servant* to rob his *master*, than for a *stranger* ; what greater crime is it for a *servant* to kill his *master*, than in another ; why is it *capital* to steal above the value of twelve-pence privately from one's person, and only *transportation* to carry off a load of corn from an open field ; and why, in the island of Man, was it formerly only *trespass*, to take away a

horse or, an ox, and *capital misdemesnor*, to steal a pig or a fowl?   16.

25. What is the sentiment of the Marquis Beccaria, as to *severity* of *punishment?*   17.

26. What does a multitude of sanguinary laws argue in a government?   17.

27. What is the evil of making no distinction in the nature and gradations of *punishment?*   18.

28. How many *offences* have been declared by *act of parliament, felonies, without benefit of clergy;* and why does so large a list, instead of diminishing, increase the number of *offenders?*   18, 19.

CHAP. II.

Of the Persons capable of committing Crimes.

1. To what single consideration, may all the several pleas and excuses, which protect the committer of a forbidden act from the *punishment* which is otherwise annexed thereto, be reduced?   20.

2. What two things must there be, to constitute a *crime* against human laws?   21.

3. In what three cases, does not the *will* join with act?   21.

4. What four species of defect in *will* fall under the first of these general heads; what two

under the second ; and what two under the third ?   21, 22.

5. In what cases, does the law privilege an *infant*, under the age of twenty-one years ; and in what under the age of fourteen only ?   22.

6. By what is the capacity of doing ill measured, as the law has stood since the time of Edward the Third ?   23.

7. At what age may an *infant* be guilty of *felony ;* and though *prima facie,* an *infant* shall be adjudged to be *doli incapax* under fourteen, yet with what *proviso,* may he be convicted and suffer *death* under that age ?   23, 24.

8. What is the rule of law as to *lunatics,* which may be easily adapted also to *idiots?*   24.

9. If a man, in his sound memory, commit an *offence,* and before *arraignment* for it, he become *mad,* why shall not he be *arraigned* for it ; if after he have *pleaded,* he becomes *mad,* why shall he not be *tried ;* if after he be *tried* and found *guilty,* why shall not *judgment* be pronounced ; and, if after *judgment,* why shall *execution* be stayed ?   **24.**

10. But what, if there be any doubt whether the *party* be *compos,* or not ; and what, if a *lunatic* have lucid intervals of understanding ?   25.

11. How may madmen be restrained from going loose ?   25.

12. Does drunkenness excuse a crime ?   25, 26.

13. When is a man, who commits an unlawful act by misfortune or chance, excused from all guilt?   26, 27.

4. What ignorance or mistake excuses crime?   27.

15. What are the three species of necessity or compulsion, which excuse crime?   28. 30.

16. When only is the constraint of a superior in a private relation allowed as an excuse for what crimes?   28, 29.

17. Why shall no plea of coverture, or presumption of the *husband's* coercion, excuse the *wife* in case of treason?   29.

18. In what one offence may a *wife* be indicted, and set in the pillory *with* her *husband;* and why? 29.

19. For what offences only is *duress per minas* an excuse?   30.

20. If a man be violently assaulted, and have no other possible means of escaping death, but by killing an innocent person, whom may he kill?   30.

21. Where a man, by the commandment of the law, is bound to arrest another for any capital offence, or to disperse a riot, and resistance is made to his authority, whom may he even kill, and why?   31.

22. May a man, in extreme want of food or cloathing justify stealing either to relieve his present necessities?   31, 32.

23. What one case is there, in which the *law* supposes an incapacity of doing wrongs from the excellence and perfection of the *person?* 32, 33.

CHAP. III.

Of Principals and Accessories.

1. WHAT are the two different degrees of *guilt* among persons that are capable of offending ? 34.
2. In what two degrees, may a man be *principal* in an *offence?* 34.
3. Must the *principal* in the second degree be actually immediately standing by, within sight or hearing of the fact? 34.
4. In cases of *murder* committed in the absence of the *murderer,* by means which he had prepared beforehand, is the *murderer principal* in the first or second degree, or *accessory;* and why? 34, 35.
5. Who is an *accessory;* and of what two kinds are *accessories?* 35.
6. Why are all *principals,* in *high treason?* 35.
7. In what crimes, may there be *accessories?* 36.
8. Why are all *principals,* in *petit larceny,* and in all crimes under the degree of *felony?* 36.
9. If a *servant* instigate a stranger to kill his

master, is he guilty of being *accessory* to *petty treason ?*   36.

10. Who is an *accessory before the fact ?*   36, 37.

11. If A. command B. to beat C. and B. beat him so that he die, is A. *accessory* to the *murder ?*   37.

12. If A. command B. to burn C 's house and he, in so doing, commit a *robbery*, is A. *accessory* to the *robbery ?*   37.

13. If A. command B. to poison C. and B. stab or shoot him, is A. *accessory* to the *murder ?*   37.

14. Who is an *accessory after the fact ;* and what two things are necessary to make one ? 37, 38.

15. Does the relief of a *felon* in gaol, with cloaths or other necessaries, make a man an *accessory after the fact ?*   38.

16. Who are made *accessories* (when the *principal felony* admits of *accessories*) by the statutes, 5 Ann. c. 31., and 4 Geo. I. c. 11. ?   38.

17. What, if one wound another mortally, and before death ensue, a person assist or receive the delinquent ?   38.

18. What, if the *parent* assist or relieve the *child*, the *child* the *parent*, the *brother* the *brother*, the *master* the *servant*, the *servant* the *master*, the *husband* the *wife*, or the *wife* the *husband*, who have any of them committed a *felony ?*   38, 39.

19. How are *accessories* to be treated, considered distinct from *principals ?*   39.

20. For what four reasons, then, are such elaborate distinctions made between *accessories* and
principals?   39, 40.

21. In what cases are *accessories after the fact*, by
the statutes, still allowed the *benefit of clergy ;*
and in what cases, is that *benefit of clergy* denied to the *principals*, and *accessories before
the fact?*   39.

22. Is an *acquittal* of receiving or counselling a
felon an *acquittal* of the *felony* itself?   40.

23. Can one, *acquitted* as *principal*, be *indicted*, as
an *accessory* either *before*, or *after*, *the fact?*
40.

CHAP. IV.

Of Offences against God and Religion.

1. OF what five species, are *crimes* and *misdemesnors*, which are either directly or by consequence injurious to *civil* society, and therefore punishable by the laws of England?
42, 43.

2. Of such *crimes* and *misdemesnors*, as more immediately offend Almighty God, by openly
transgressing the precepts of religion either
natural or revealed, what constitutes that
guilt in the action, which human tribunals
are to censure?   43.

3. What eleven crimes are of this species?   43,
44. 50. 59, 60. 62—64.

4. What is *apostasy;* and in whom only can it take place? 43.

5. As a penalty for *apostasy*, what is enacted by statute 9 & 10 W. III. c. 32. ? 44.

6. What is *heresy;* what was the writ *de hæretico comburendo ;* what did the statute 29 Car. II. as to *heresy;* and, as a penalty for *heresy*, what is enacted by the statute 9 & 10 W. III. ? 44—46. 49, 50.

7. Of what two kinds are the *offences* against *religion*, which affect the *established church* ? 50.

8. What are the penalties for reviling the ordinances of the church, by statutes 1 Edw. VI. c. 1., and 1. Eliz cc. 1. & 2. ? 50, 51.

9. Of what two classes are *non-conformists ;* what penalties are imposed upon those of the first class, by statutes 1 Eliz. c. 2., 23. Eliz. c. 1., and 3 Jac. I. c. 4.; and what are suspended by the statute 1 W. & M. st. 1. c. 18., commonly called the *toleration act*, confirmed by statute 10 Ann. c. 2., from which of those of the second class, with what three *provisoes* ? 52, 53.

10. What are dissenting teachers to subscribe, in order to be exempted from the penalties of the statutes of Car. II., 13 & 14 c. 4., 15 c. 6., 17 c. 2., and 22 c. I., ; and from what particular penalties of the first and third of those statutes (with what exceptions) are

28

they exempted by subscribing the declaration of the act 19 Geo. III.? 53, 54.

11. What, by the same statute 1 W. & M., if any person shall wilfully, maliciously, or contemptuously disturb any congregation, assembled in any *church* or permitted *meeting-house*, or shall misuse any preacher or teacher there? 54.

12. But what does the statute 5 Geo. I. c. 4. enact, as to any *mayor's* or principal *magistrate's* appearing at any *dissenting meeting?* 54.

13. Why do not the reasons, for a general toleration of *protestant dissenters*, hold equally strong as to *papists?* 54, 55.

14. Into what three classes, may *papists* be divided? 55.

15. What are the penalties and disabilities of the first class of *papists?* 55.

16. What, if any person send another abroad to be educated in the *popish religion*, or to reside in any *religious house* abroad for that purpose, or contribute to his maintenance when there? 55.

17. What, if these errors be aggravated by *apostasy*, or perversion? 55.

18. To what additional disabilities, penalties, and forfeitures, is the second class of *papists* subject? 56.

19. What is the effect of refusing to make the declaration against *popery*, enjoined by sta-

tute 30 Car. II. st. 2., when tendered by the proper magistrate ?   56.

20. What are the penalties against the third class of *papists ;* and of what are all persons harbouring them guilty ?   57.

21. Are these laws enforced now ; and whence is their origin ?   57.

22. In respect of whom, is the statute of 11 & 12 W. III. repealed, to what extent, by the statute 18 Geo. III. c. 60. ?   58.

23. But now, by statute 31 Geo. III. c. 32., from what *Roman catholics* are all these restrictions and penalties removed ; and how are *Roman catholic ministers, schoolmasters,* and *congregations* tolerated ?   To be answered from Mr. Justice Christian's note (1) to this chapter.   58.

24. What do the *corporation* and *test acts* enact ?   58, 59.

25. To whom does the statute 7 Jac. I. c. 2. apply a like test ?   59.

26. What is *blasphemy?* and how is it punishable at *common law* ?   59.

27. How are *profane* and *common swearing* and *cursing* punishable by the statute 19 Geo. II. c. 21. ; and what is enacted against *profanity* on the *stage,* by statute 3 Jac. 1. c. 21. ? 59, 60.

28. What is *witchcraft, conjuration, enchantment,* or *sorcery ;* and what is declared as to it by statute 9 Geo. II. c. 5. ?   60—62.

29. How is the pretence to using *witchcraft*, telling fortunes, or discovering stolen goods by skill in the occult sciences, punished? 62.

30. Who are *religious impostors;* and how are they punishable? 62.

31. Why is *simony* to be considered as an offence against *religion;* who are punishable for it by statute 31 Eliz. c. 6.; and how? 62.

32. What other corrupt elections and resignations are punished by the same statute, and how? 63.

33. What is *sabbath-breaking;* and how are what instances of it punishable by statutes, 27 Hen. VI. c.5. as to *fairs* or *markets*, 1 Car. I. c. 1., as to *unlawful exercises*, and 29 Car. II. c. 7., as to *work?* 63, 64.

34. How is *drunkenness* punished by statute 4. Jac. I. e. 5.? 64.

35. When is *lewdness* an indictable offence; and how is it punished? 64, 65.

36. In what event may who be punished for having *bastard children*, by statute 7 Jac. I. c. 4., and how? 65.

CHAP. V.

Of Offences against the Law of Nations.

1. WHAT is the *law of nations;* and upon what principle is it founded ?   66.
2. By what is this law enforced in *England?*   67.
3. What is the remedy for *offences* against this *law,* by whole *states* and *nations ?* 68.
4. What if the individuals of any *state* violate this *law?*   68.
5. What are the three principal *offences* against this *law,* animadverted on as such by the *municipal laws* of *England ?*   68.
6. How may the *violation* of *safe-conducts,* or *passports* expressly granted by the *king* or his *ambassadors* to the *subjects* of a foreign *power,* in time of mutual *war,* be punished ; and what is enacted as to *offences* against *strangers* at *sea,* or in *port,* by statute 31 Hen. VI. c. 4. ?   68—70.
7. What is enacted by the statute 7 Ann. c. 12., in order to enforce the *law of nations,* as to the *rights* of *ambassadors ?*   70, 71.
8. What is the *offence* of *piracy* by *common law ;* how only is it punishable since the *statute of treasons,* 25 Edw. III. c. 2. ; and what offences are made *piracy* by statutes 11 & 12 W. III. c. 7., 8 Geo. I. c.24., and 18 Geo. II. c. 30. ?   71—73.

CHAP. VI.

Of High Treason.

1. INTO what four kinds may those *offences* be distinguished, which more immediately affect the *royal person*, his *crown* or *dignity*, and which are, in some degree, a breach of the duty of *allegiance*, whether natural and innate, or local and acquired by residence ? 74.

2. What is *treason proditio ;* how is the appellation generally used by the *law ;* and of what two kinds is *treason ?* 74, 75.

3. Under what seven distinct branches, are all kinds of *high treason* comprehended by the statute 25 Edw. III. c. 2. ? 76. 81—84.

4. Is a *queen regnant,* or a *king consort,* within the words of the *act ;* is a *king de facto,* and not *de jure ;* is a *king de jure,* and not *de facto ;* what is the true construction of the statute 11 Hen. VII. c. 1. ; and is a *king* who has resigned his *crown,* abdicated his *government* or subverted the *constitution,* any longer the object of *treason ?* 76—78.

5. What is *compassing* or *imagining* the death of the *king ;* and how must this act of the mind be demonstrated, before it can possibly fall under any judicial cognizance ? 78, 79.

6. What are held to be *overt acts* of *treason* in *imagining* the *king's* death ? 79.

7. Are *words spoken, treason ?* 80.

8. Are *words written, treason?*   81.

9. What does the phrase, " the *king's companion,*" mean to violate whom is declared, by the statute, to be the second species of *treason ;* and when is it *treason* in both *parties?*   81.

10. What is held as to the violation of a *queen,* or *princess dowager ;* and why ?   81.

11. What *offences* of *taking up arms,* does the third species of *treason* include ?   81, 82.

12. To what does an *insurrection* to pull down *all inclosures, all brothels,* and the like amount ; and to what does a tumult to pull down *a particular house,* or lay open *a particular inclosure ?*   82.

13. What, if two *subjects* quarrel and levy *war* against each other ?   82.

14. When does a bare *conspiracy* to levy *war* amount to *treason?*   82.

15. How must the fourth species of treason, or that of adherence to the *king's* enemies, be proved ?   82.

16. In what light, is giving assistance to foreign *pirates* or *robbers, treason ?*   83.

17. Under what description, is adherence or aid to our own fellow-subjects in actual rebellion at home, *treason ?*   83.

18. What is held, as to relieving a *rebel* fled out of the kingdom ; and why ?   83.

19. In what events shall a man's joining with either *rebels* or *enemies, in* the kingdom, be excused ?   83.

20. To what offence does the taking wax, which bears the impression of the *great seal*, off from one *patent* and affixing it on another, amount?   83, 84.

21. What *money* is meant by the statute, to counterfeit which is the sixth species of *treason?* 84.

22. Which of the *king's officers* of *justice* are within the statute, which declares the " slaying of them in their places doing their offices," *treason?*   84.

23. What does the *act* say, as to " other like cases of *treason* or *constructive treasons?*   85.

24. Under what three heads, are comprized the *high treasons* created by subsequent statutes, and not comprehended under the description of statute 25 Edw. III. ?   87.

25. In what three cases relating to *papists*, is the offence of *high treason* declared to be committed, by the statutes 5 Eliz. c. 1., 27 Eliz. c. 2., and 3 Jac. l. c. 4. ; and what is the reason of distinguishing these *overt acts* of *popery* from all others, which were considered in a preceding chapter as *spiritual offences?*   87, 88.

26. With regard to *treasons* relative to the *coin*, or other *royal signatures*, what two *offences* are declared to be *high treason* by statute 1 Mar. st. 2. c. 6. ; and what one in consequence of the former, with regard to *importing coin*, by statute 1 & 2 P. M. c. 11.?   89.

27. Is it *high treason* to counterfeit foreign money, taken here by consent ?   89.

28. What instances of *falsifying* the *coin* are declared to be *high treason*, by statutes 5 Eliz. c. 11., and 18 Eliz. c. 12.? 90.

29. What *offences*, as to implements of, and preparations for coinage, are declared to be *high treason*, by statute 8 & 9 W III. c. 26., made perpetual by 7 Ann. c. 25.; and within what times, must all prosecutions on this *act* be commenced? 90.

30. What species of *coining* is made *high treason* by statute 15 & 16 Geo. II. c. 28.; but in what case shall the offender be pardoned? 90, 91.

31. What *offences* are made *high treason*, with a view to the security of the *protestant succession*, with regard to the late *Pretender* or his sons, by statutes 13 & 14 W. III. c. 3., and 17 G. II. c. 39., and generally by statutes 1 Ann. st. 2. c. 17., and 6 Ann. c. 7.? 91, 92.

32. What *offences* are made *high treason* by the statute 33 Geo. III. c. 27., called the *traiterous correspondence act*; and what else does the statute enact? To be answered from Mr. Justice Christian's note (9) to this chapter. 92.

33. Of what six parts does the *punishment* for *high treason* consist; but what parts may be discharged by the *king*? 92, 93.

34. How is the *punishment* milder for *male offenders*, in case of *coining*? 93.

35. But what is the *punishment* of *females*, in *treasons* of every kind? 93.

29

CHAP. VII.

Of Felonies injurious to the King's Prerogative.

1. WHAT is *felony*, in the general acceptation of our *English law?*   94, 95.

2. What is the etymology of the word, according to Sir Henry Spelman; how is this etymology confirmed by the feodal writers; and wherefore are *suicide, homicide, petit larceny, robbery, rape,* and *treason, felonies,* by the antient law?   95—97.

3. As there are *felonies* without *capital punishment,* may *capital punishments* be inflicted where the *offence* is no *felony?*   97.

4. But to what usage, do the interpretations of the *law* now conform ; and in compliance therewith, in what light does the present *commentator* intend to consider *felony?*   98.

5. Of what five kinds, are such *felonies* as are more immediately injurious to the *King's prerogative?*   98.

6. Of the various *offences* relating to the *coin,* as well *misdemesnors* as *felonies,* declared by a series of statutes, what are the several penalties for melting down sterling money, by statute 9 Edw. III. st. 2.; for melting down current silver money, by statute 13 & 14 Car. II. c. 31. ; for importing false *money;* for forging any foreign *coin,* although it be not

made current here by *proclamation*; for having to do with *clippings* or *filings* of the
coin, for blanching *copper* for sale, or dealing
in any malleable composition resembling
gold, or buying at a less rate than it imports.
to be of, any counterfeit or diminished milled
money of this kingdom, not being cut in
pieces (an operation which is, in what case,
directed, and, in what cases, allowed and required, by certain statutes, to be performed);
for tendering any counterfeit *coin*, knowing it
to be so; for doing so, having more in custody, or repeating the offence within ten days
after; and for counterfeiting copper half-
pence or farthings, or dealing in it (not
being cut in pieces or melted) at a less
value than it imports to be of? 98—100.

7. What is enacted by statute 3 Hen. VII.
c. 14. and 9 Ann. c. 16., as to *felonies*
against the *king's council?* 100, 101.

8. In what cases is it made *felony* to serve
foreign *states*, by statutes 3 Jac. I. c. 4.,
9 Geo. II. c. 30., and 29 Geo. II. c. 17?
101.

9. What is enacted by the statute 31 Eliz. c. 4., as
to *felony* in embezzling the *king's* armour or
warlike stores; what effect upon this statute
has that of 22 Car. II. c. 5.; how are other
inferior embezzlements and *misdemesnors*
punished by several statutes; and what is

enacted by statute 12 Geo. III. c. 24. ?
101, 102.

10. What is enacted by statutes 18 Hen. VI.
c. 19., and 5 Eliz. c. 5., as to desertion from
the *king's armies* in time of *war*, whether by
land or sea ; what effect upon this statute has
that of 2 & 3 Edw. VI. c. 2. ; and how are
other inferior *military offences* punishable by
the same statutes ?   102.

─────

CHAP. VIII.

Of Præmunire.

1. WHY is the *offence* of *præmunire* so called ;
and whence did it take its original ?   103.
2. What does the *statute of præmunire* 16 Ric. II.
c. 5. enact ; and who are also subjected to the
penalties of *præmunire* by statute 2 Hen. IV.
c. 3. ?   112.
3. What *offences* are made liable to the pains of
præmunire, by the statutes of Hen. VIII. and
Eliz. ?   115.
4. To what penalty is the importing or selling
mass-books, or other *popish books* liable by
statute 3 Jac. I. c. 5. § 25. ?   115.
5. To what twelve other *offences*, some of which
bear no relation to the original *offence*, have
the penalties of *præmunire* been applied by
various statutes ?   116, 117.

6. How is the *punishment* of *præmunire* shortly summed up by Sir Edward Coke; except in the case of transgressing what statute, may the *king*, by his *prerogative*, remit the whole or any part of the *punishment;* and what does the statute 5 Eliz. c. 1. provide as to the consequences of an *attaint* by *præmunire?* 117, 118.

CHAP. IX.

Of Misprisions and Contempts, affecting the King and Government.

1. WHAT are *misprisions (mespris)*, and *contempts;* and of what two sorts? 119.
2. Of what three kinds are *negative misprisions?* 120, 121.
3. What is *misprision of treason;* but what circumstances make this offender guilty of *high treason?* 120.
4. What positive *misprision of treason* is created by statute 13 Eliz. c. 2.? 120.
5. What is the *punishment* for *misprision of treason?* 120.
6. What is *misprision of felony;* and how is it punished by the statute Westm. 1., 3 Edw. I. c. 9.? 121.

7. What is the *punishment* for *misprision* of *trea-sure-trove?* 121.

8. Of what five kinds are *positive misprisions,* or *contempts* and *high misdemesnors,* the last four consisting, in general, of such *contempts* of the *executive magistrate,* as demonstrate themselves by some arrogant and undutiful behaviour towards the *king* and *government?* 121—124.

9. What *offences* are included under the *misprision* of the *mal-administration* of such high officers as are in public trust and employment; and how is it usually punished? 121, 122.

10. What are *contempts* against the *king's pre-rogative?* 122.

11. Whose duty is it, and when, to join the *posse comitatus,* or *power of the county,* according to the statute 2 Hen. V. c. 8.? 122.

12. How are *contempts* against the *King's pre-rogative* punished? 122.

13. What are *contempts* and *misprisions* against the *king's person* and *government;* and how may they be punished? 123.

14. What are *contempts* against the *king's title,* not amounting to *treason* or *præmunire;* and how are they punished? 123.

15. What *offence* is it, and how punishable by statute 13 Eliz. c. 1., to maintain that the *common laws* of this realm, not altered by

parliament, ought not to direct the right of the*crown of *England*?   123.

16. What are the penalties inflicted by statute 1 Geo. I. st. 2. c. 13., for refusing or neglecting to take the *oaths* appointed by *statute for better securing the government*, and yet acting or serving in a public office, place of trust, or other capacity, for which the said oaths are required to be taken ; and what, if *members* on the *foundation* of any *college* in the two *universities*, who, by this statute, are bound to take the *oaths*, do not register a *certificate* thereof in the *college-register*, within one month after ?   123, 124.

17. What are *contempts* against the *king's palaces* or *courts of justice*; and how are they, a *rescue* from them, and an *affray*, or *riot* near them, but out of their actual view, punishable ?   124, 125.

18. How are threatening or reproachful words to any *judge*, sitting in the *courts*, punishable ; and how is an *affray*, or *contemptuous behaviour*, in the *inferior courts* of the *King* ? 126.

19. How are such as are guilty of any injurious treatment to those, who are immediately under the protection of a *court of justice*, punishable ?   126.

20. How are endeavours to dissuade a *witness* from giving *evidence*, disclosures of examination

before a *privy council*, advice to a *prisoner* to
stand mute, or disclosures by one of the
grand jury to any person indicted of the
evidence against him, construed and punished? 126.

CHAP. X.

Of Offences against public Justice.

1. INTO what five species, may those *crimes* and
mesdemesnors, that more especially affect the
commonwealth, be divided? 127, 128.
2. What are the twenty-two *offences* against *public
justice*, beginning with those that are most
penal, and descending gradually to such as
are of less malignity? 128—137. 139—141.
3. What is enacted by statute 8 Hen. VI. c. 12.,
as to embezzling or vacating *records*, by
statute 21 Jac. I. c. 26., as to acknowledging
any *proceedings* in the *courts* in the name of
another person, not privy to the same, and
by statute 4 W. & M. c. 4., as to personating
any other person as *bail?* 128.
4. What is enacted by statute 14 Edw. III. c. 10.,
if any gaoler compel any *prisoner* to become
an *approver* or an *appellor?* 128, 129.
5. What is the *offence* of obstructing the *execution*
of lawful *process* in *criminal cases;* and what is
enacted by several statutes, as to opposing the

execution of any process in pretended privileged places within the *bills of mortality?*
129.

6. Who are punishable for the *escape* of a person arrested upon *criminal process*, how, and
when?   129, 130.

7. How is *breach of prison* by the *offender* himself,
punished by the statute *de frangentibus pri-
sonam*, 1 Edw. II.?   130, 131.

8. What is *rescue ;* how is it punishable, and
when ; what is enacted by statutes 11 Geo. II.
c. 26., and 24 Geo. II. c. 40., as to *rescues* of
any retailers of spirituous liquors, and by
statute 16 Geo. II. c. 31., as to assisting *prisoners* to escape ; and what, if any person be
charged with any of the *offences* against the
black-act 9 Geo. I. c. 22., and being required
by order of the *privy-council* to surrender himself, neglect to do so for 40 days?   131.

9. Who are punishable for an *offender*'s returning
from *transportation*, and how?   132.

10. What is enacted by statute 4 Geo. I. c. 11.,
as to the *offence* of taking a reward, under
pretence of helping the owner to his stolen
goods?   132.

11. In the *offence* of receiving stolen goods knowing them to be stolen, which makes the *offender
accessary* to the theft, of what other punishment has the *prosecutor*, by statute 1 Ann.
c. 9., and 5 Ann. c. 31., the choice, before
the thief be taken and convicted ; and what

is enacted as to receivers and possessors of certain metals, by statute 29 Geo. II. c. 30., and as to knowing receivers of stolen plate or jewels taken by *highway-robbery* or *bur-glary?* 182, 133.

13. What is *theft-bote*, and how is it punished ; and what is enacted by statute 25 Geo. II. c. 36., as to advertising a reward for the re-return of things stolen, with " no questions asked ?" 133, 134.

13. What is *common barretry ;* how is it punished and what is enacted by statute 12 Geo. I. c. 29., in case an *attorney* shall have been con-victed of this *offence ?* 134.

14. What is the punishment for *suing* in a false name in the *superior courts ;* and what in the *inferior*, by statute 8 Eliz. c. 2., ? 134.

15. What is the *offence* of *maintenance ;* when is it not an offence ; and what is the *punishment* for it, when it is by *common law*, and by sta-tute 32 Hen. VIII. c. 9. ? 134, 135.

16. What is *champerty (campi partitio) ;* and what has the *law*'s abhorrence of it led it to say of a *chose in action* by *common law*, and of a pretended *right* or *title* to *land*, by statute 32 Hen. VIII. c. 9. ? 135, 136.

17. What is enacted by statute 18 Eliz. c. 5., as to compounding *informations* upon *penal sta-tutes?* 136.

18. In what two ways may conspirators to indict

an innocent man of *felony* be punished ?
136, 137.

19. How àre threats of accusation, in order to
extort money, punishable by statute 30
Geo. II. c. 24. ?   137.

20. How is *perjury* defined by Sir Edward Coke ;
what is *subornation* of *perjury ;* how are they
now punished at *common law*, with an added power in the court to inflict what penalties, by statute 2 Geo. II. c. 25. ; and how
may they be punished by statute 5 Eliz. c. 9. ?
137, 138.

21. When is *bribery* an *offence* against *public justice ;* in whom and how is it punished ; and
what is enacted on 'this subject by a statute 11
Hen. IV. ?   139, 140.

22. What is *embracery ;* and in whom and how is
it punished ?   140.

23 How was the *false verdict* of *jurors* antiently
considered, and how punished ?   140.

24. In what *public officers* is negligence an *offence*
against *public justice ;* and how is it punishable ?   140.

25. How is the oppression and tyrannical partiality of *magistrates* prosecuted and punished ?   141.

26. When is extortion an abuse of *public justice ;*
and what is the punishment for it ?   141.

CHAP. XI.

Of Offences against the Public Peace.

1. Of what two species are *offences* against the *public peace*, and of what two degrees, are both these kinds ?   142.

2. What are the thirteen kinds of *offences* against the *public peace* ?   142—150.

3. What does the statute 1 Geo. I. c. 5. enact, as to the riotous assembling of twelve persons, or more, and not dispersing upon proclamation ?   143.

4. What does the statute 9 Geo. I. c. 22. enact, as to appearing armed, or hunting in disguise ?   143, 144.

5. What does the same statute amended by statute 27 Geo. II. c. 15., enact, as to sending any demanding or threatening letter ?   144.

6. What, by several late statutes, are the penalties for destroying or damaging any *lock*, *sluice* or *flood-gate*, or any *turnpike-gate*, or its appurtenances, or for rescuing such destroyers or damagers ?   144, 145.

7. What are *affrays (affraier)* ; wherein do they differ from *assaults* ; by whom, and how, may they be suppressed ; and what is their punishment ?   145.

8. What is enacted by statute 5 & 6 Edw. VI. c, 4., as to *affrays* in a *church* or *church-yard* ?   146.

9. What are *riots, routs,* and *unlawful assemblies;* and of how many persons must they be con- stituted; how are they punished by *common law;* and what is enacted for their suppres- sion, by statute 13 Hen. IV. c. 7.? 146, 147.

10. What is *tumultuous petitioning;* and what is enacted, for its prevention, by statute 13 Car. II. st. 1. c. 5.? 147, 148.

11. What is *forcible entry* or *detainer;* and how, by several statutes, may it be suppressed and punished? 148, 149.

12. What is the *offence* of going unusually armed; and how is it prohibited by the statute of Northampton, 2 Edw. III. c. 3.? 149.

13. When is the *offence* of spreading false news punishable, and how? 149.

14. How is the *offence* of *pretended prophecy* punished by statute 5 Eliz. c. 15.? 149.

15. In whom are challenges to fight punishable, and how; and what, by statute 9 Ann. c. 14., if the challenge, or any *assault* or *affray,* arise on account of any money won at gaming? 150.

16. What are *libels,* which tend to the breach of the peace; what is a publication of them, in the eye of the *law;* what if they be true, and what if they be false; what is the dif- ference between a *libel* in a *civil action,* and a *libel* in a *criminal prosecution;* and what is the punishment of *criminal libels?* 150, 151.

17. Though it have been long held that the truth of a *libel* is no justification, in a *criminal prosecution*, yet what general rule has the *court* of *king's bench* laid down, as to granting an *information* for a *libel?* To be answered from Mr. J. Christian's note (5) to this chapter. 151.

CHAP. XII.

Of Offences against Public Trade.

1. OF what two degrees are *offences* against *public trade?*   154.

2. What are the thirteen kinds of these *offences?* 154. 156—160.

3. What is *owling;* and what are its penalties, by several statutes?   154.

4. What is *smuggling;* and how is it punished by statute 19 Geo. II. c. 34.?   154, 155.

5. What are the several species of *fraudulent bankruptcy,* taken notice of by the *statute law;* and how are they punished?   156.

6. What, by statute 21 Jac. I. c. 19., if the *bankrupt* cannot make it appear, that he is disabled from paying his *debts* by some casual loss; and what, by statute 32 Geo. II. c. 28., and 33 Geo. III. c. 5., if a prisoner charged

in execution for *debt* (to what amount ?) neglect or refuse on demand to deliver up his *effects?* 156., and see Mr. J. Christian's note (3) at this page.

7. What is the penalty for *usury;* what, if any scrivener or broker take more than five shillings *per cent. procuration-money,* or more than twelve-pence for making a *bond;* and what is enacted, on this subject, by statute 17 Geo. III. c. 26. ? 156, 157.

8. What *offences* may be referred to the head of *cheating;* what is the general punishment for all frauds of this kind, if indicted at *common law;* and what frauds are punished by the statutes 33 Hen. VIII. c. I., and 30 Geo. II. c. 24. ? 157, 158.

9. How are the three *offences* of *forestalling, regrating,* and *engrossing,* described by statute 5 & 6 Edw. VI. c. 14.; and what is the general penalty for these offences by *common law?* 158, 159.

10. What are *monopolies;* and how are they punished? 159.

11. How are combinations among victuallers or artificers, to raise the prices of commodities, punished by statute 2 & 3 Edw. VI. c. 15. ? 159, 160.

12. How is the *offence* of exercising a trade without having served an apprenticeship punished by statute 5 Eliz. c. 4. ? 160.

13. What is enacted, by several statutes of Geo. II,

and Geo. III., to prevent the seduction of our artists abroad, and the destruction of our home manufactures ? 160., and Mr. J. Christian's note (8) at the same page.

***

CHAP. XIII.

Of Offences against the Public Health, and the Public Police or Œconomy.

1. What are the two *offences* against the public health of the nation ? 161, 162.
2. What is enacted by statute 1 Jac. 1. c. 31., as to any person infected with the *plague*, or dwelling in any infected house ; and what is the present *law*, as to *quarantine?* 161, 162.
3. What is enacted by statutes 51 Hen. III. st. 6. and 12 Car. II. c. 25. § 11. to prevent the selling of unwholesome provisions and wine ? 162.
4. What is meant by the *public peace and œconomy?* 162.
5. What are the nine *offences* against the *public peace and œconomy?* 162—166. 169—171. 174.
6. What is enacted by the statute 26 Geo. II. c. 33., for the prevention of the *offence* of *clandestine marriages?* 162, 163.
7. What is *bigamy*, or more properly *polygamy;*

what is its effect upon the *second marriage;* and how is it punished by statute 1 Jac. I. c. 11., with an exception to what five cases ? 163, 164.

8. How are wandering *soldiers* and *mariners,* or persons pretending so to be, punished by statute 39 Eliz. c. 17. ? 164, 165.

9. How are persons calling themselves *Egyptians,* or *gypsies,* now punished by statute 23 Geo. III. c. 51. ? To be answered from Mr. J. Christian's note (6) to this chapter. 167.

10. What are *common nusances,* and of what seven sorts ? 167, 168.

11. Who may be *indicted,* and what shall be equivalent to such *indictment,* for annoyances in *highways, bridges,* and public *rivers,* whether by positive obstructions, or want of reparation ; and what is a *purpresture ?* 167.

12. What if *inn-keepers* refuse to entertain a *traveller,* without a very sufficient cause ? 167.

13. How may *eaves-droppers* be punished ? 168.

14. How may a *common scold (communis rixatrix) ?* 168.

15. Into what three classes are *idle persons* divided, and how is each class punished by stat. 17 Geo. II. c. 5. ; and to what are persons harbouring *vagrants* liable ? 169, 170.

16. What one sumptuary *law* against *luxury* is still unrepealed ? 170.

17. What is enacted by statute 16 Car. II. c. 7., if

31

any person by playing, or betting, shall lose more than 100l. at one time; what does the statute 9 Ann. c. 14. enact, as to all securities given for money won at play, if any person at one sitting lose 10l. at play, and if any person, by cheating at play, win the same sum ; what does the statute 13 Geo. II. c. 19. enact to prevent the multiplicity of *horse-races ;* and what, by statute 18 Geo. II. c. 34 , if any person win or lose at play, or by betting 10l. at one time, or 20l. within twenty-four hours ? 172, 173.

18. Who are guilty of the *offence* of destroying the *game* upon the old principles of the *forest-law,* and who, by the *game-laws ;* and what are the four *qualifications* for killing game, as they are usually called, or, more properly, the exemptions from the penalties inflicted by the *statute-law ?* 174, 175.

19. What are the punishments for *unqualified persons* transgressing the *game-laws,* in what ways ; and how may those punishments be inflicted ? 175.

20. What is enacted for the preservation of *game* by statute 28 Geo. II. c. 12. ? 175.

CHAP. XIV.

Of Homicide.

1. OF what three principal kinds, are those *crimes* and *misdemesnors*, which in a more peculiar manner, affect and injure individuals, or *private subjects?* 177.

2. Of *crimes* injurious to the *persons* of *private subjects*, what is the most principal and important? 177.

3. Of what three kinds, and of what three degrees of guilt, is *homicide?* 177, 178.

4. In what three cases is *homicide justifiable?* 178, 179.

5. What *offence* is it wantonly to kill the greatest of malefactors? 178.

6. What, if *judgment* of *death* be given by a *judge* not authorized by lawful commission, and *execution* be done accordingly? 178.

7. What if even the *judge* execute his own *judgment*; and what if an *officer* behead one who is adjudged to be hanged, or *vice versâ?* 179.

8. Of what six kinds are *justifiable homicides*, committed for the advancement of *public justice?* 179, 180.

9. But in all these first five cases, what apparent necessity must there be on the *officer's* side? 180.

10. When is it lawful to kill any person who attempts a *burglary;* and what is the uniform

principle that runs through all *laws* as to re-
pelling *crimes* by *homicide?* 180, 181.

11. What is Mr. Locke's doctrine on this subject,
and how is it received by the *commentator?* 181, 182.

12. Wherein does *excusable*, differ from *justifiable
homicide;* and of what two sorts is the former? 182.

13. In what cases does homicide *per infortunium*,
or *misadventure* happen? 182.

14. In what cases, however, is the slayer guilty of
manslaughter, and not *misadventure* only;
but when are deaths in *tilts* or *tournaments*,
boxing or *sword-playing*, only *misadventure?*
183.

15. What is *homicide* in *self-defence*, or *se defendendo;* what is *chance-medley*, or *chaud-
medley;* and what must appear to excuse
homicide by the *plea* of *self-defence?*

16. What seems to be the true criterion to distin-
tinguish *homicide* upon *chance-medley*, in *self-
defence*, from *manslaughter* in the legal sense
of the word? 184, 185.

17. What *civil* and *natural relations* are comprehended under the excuse of *se defendendo*,
and why? 186.

18. Is there not one species of *homicide se defendendo*, where the party slain is equally innocent with him who occasions his death;
and upon what principle is this *homicide* excusable? 186.

19. In what circumstances, do the two species of *homicide*, by *misadventure* and *self-defence*, agree ; and what does the law's high value for the life of a man always intend ? 186, 187.

20. What is the penalty for *homicide?* 188.

21. What is *felonious homicide*, and of what two kinds? 188.

22. What is *self-murder*, or *felo de se ;* does it admit of *accessories ;* when, and in whom, may it happen, and when in a real *lunatic?* 189, 190.

23. How is *self-murder* punished ? 190.

24. What, if a *husband* and *wife* be possessed jointly of a *term* of *years* in *land*, and the *husband* drown himself ; and why ? 190.

25. How do the two degrees of guilt in *killing another* divide the *offence ;* and what is the difference between either division of it ? 190.

26. How is *manslaughter* therefore defined ; and of what two branches is it ? 191.

27. When is it *voluntary manslaughter ;* and what circumstance makes it amount to *murder?* 191.

28. In what, therefore, does *voluntary manslaughter* differ from *excusable homicide, se defendendo?* 192.

29. In what does *involuntary manslaughter* differ from *homicide excusable by misadventure?* 192.

30. But what circumstances will make *involuntary manslaughter* amount to *murder*? 192, 193.

31. What is the punishment of *manslaughter*? 193.

32. But is there not one species of *manslaughter,* which is punished as *murder* by statute 1 Jac. I. c. 8.; and how is this statute construed? 193, 194,

33. How is *murder* defined, or rather described, by Sir Edward Coke? 195.

34. What if a person be indicted for one species of killing, or for killing with one weapon, and it proves to have been another? 196.

35. May a man be guilty of *murder*, although no stroke be struck by himself, or no killing primarily intended? 196.

36. Within what time after the stroke received, must the party die, in order to make the killing *murder*? 197.

37. When is it *murder* to kill a *child* in its *mother's* womb; and what is enacted by the statute 21 Jac. I. c. 27., as to a *mother's* concealing the death of her *bastard child;* but what is now required, upon *trials* for this *offence?* 198.

38. What constitutes *malice, prepense, malitia, præcogitata;* and when is *malice express,* and when *implied,* in *law?* 198—201.

39. Who are guilty of *murder*, in *deliberate duelling?* 199.

40. If two or more come together to do an un-

lawful act against the *king's peace*, and one of them kill a man, in whom is it *murder*? 200.

41. What if one intend to do another *felony*, and undesignedly kill a third man? 201.

42. Unless in what cases, may it be taken for a general rule that all *homicide* is *malicious*? 201.

43. What is the punishment of *murder*; and what is enacted, on that subject, by statute 25 Geo. II. c. 37.? 201, 202.

44. What is *petit treason (parva proditio)*; and by what three ways may it happen according to statute 25 Edw. III. c. 2.? 203.

45. Of what crime is a *servant* guilty who kills his *master* whom he has left, upon a grudge conceived against him during service; and whom is it *petit treason* in a *clergyman* to kill? 203.

46. May a person indicted of *petit treason* be found guilty of *manslaughter* or *murder*; and how many witnesses are necessary in case of *petit treason*? 204.

47. What is the punishment for *petit treason*, and what in a *woman* by statute 30 Geo III. c. 48.? 204., and see Mr. J. Christian's note (7) at the same page.

48. What is the punishment for the aiders, abettors, and counsellors, of *petit treason*? 204.

CHAP. XV.

Of Offences against the Persons of Individuals.

1. OF what two degrees of guilt, are other *offences* against the persons of individuals ? 205.
2. What are the four *felonies* ? 205. 208. 210. 215.
3. What amounts to *mayhem, mayhemium* ; and how is it punished by statutes 5 Hen. IV. c. 5., 37 Hen. VIII. c. 6., and 22 & 23 Car. II· c. 1., called the *Coventry* act ? 205—207.
4. What is enacted by statute 9 Geo. I. c. 22., as to the offence of maliciously shooting at any person ? 207.
5. What is enacted by statutes 3 Hen. VII. c. 2., and 39 Eliz. c. 9., as to the *offence* of forcible *abduction* and *marriage* of a *female*, or, as it is vulgarly called, *stealing an heiress ?* 208.
6. What four things have been determined, in the construction of the first of these statutes ; what has been determined as to the *will* of the *woman ?* and what general rule of *law* may be violated, in punishing this *offence ?* 208, 209.
7. What is enacted by the statutes 4 & 5 Ph. & M. c. 8., and 26 Geo. II. c. 33., as to an inferior degree of the same kind of *offence ?* 209, 210.
8. What is the crime of *rape ;* and what is enacted as to its punishment by statute 18 Eliz. c. 7.? 210. 212.

9. Who is presumed by the law incapable to commit a *rape?*   212.

10. Can a *rape* be committed upon a *concubine* or *harlot?*   212, 213.

11. What has been determined as to the competency and credibility of *witnesses* upon an *indictment* of *rape;* and what has been now settled as to hearsay evidence of the declarations of a *child,* who hath not capacity to be sworn?   213, 214.

12. What is the punishment for the *crime against nature?*   215, 216.

13. What are the five inferior *offences* or *misdemesnors* against the *personal security* of the *subject?*   216.

14. What are the public penalties for *assault, battery,* and *wounding;* what other ignominious corporal penalties are inflicted, in the case of *assaults* with intent to *murder,* or to commit either of the *crimes* last spoken of; and, when both parties are consenting to the last *crime,* what is it usual to charge?   216, 217.

15. What is enacted by the statute called *articuli cleri,* 9 Edw. II. c. 3., as to the offence of *beating* a *clerk* in *orders?*   217, 218.

16. As to the public *offence* of *false imprisonment,* how is the sending any *subject* of this realm a *prisoner* beyond the seas punished; what does the statute 43 Eliz. c. 13. declare as to this kind of *offence* in the four northern counties; and how are inferior degrees of

32

—

CHAP. XVI.

Of Offences against the Habitations of Individuals.

he is not permitted to do in any other case ;
and how is a *burglar* defined by Sir Edward
Coke ?   223, 224.

9. At what *time* must the *burglary* be committed,
and what is held as to the *light* by which it
is committed ?   224.

10. What is Sir Edward Coke's definition of
the place in which a burglary must be committed ; and why does it not seem extensive enough ; and when may a *burglary* be
committed in a *barn, stable* or *warehouse ?*
224, 225.

11. When is a *lodging* the *mansion-house* of the
lodger ; and can *burglary* be committed in
the *shop*, parcel of another man's *house*,
which I hire to work or trade, but not to lie
in, or in a *tent* or *booth* erected in a *market* or
fair, in which I do lodge ?   225, 226.

12. As to the manner of committing *burglary*,
what must there be to complete the *offence ;*
and what if a hole be broken one night, and
the same breakers enter the next night through
the same ?   226.

13. In what cases may *burglary* be committed,
without *breaking*, or *loosing* of *fastenings?*
226, 227.

14. What is sufficient to constitute the *entry*, which
is *burglarious ;* and what is declared as to the
precedence of the *entry* and the *burglary*, by
statute 12 Ann. c. 7. ?   227.

15. What is the law, as to the *intent* of *burglary* ? 227, 228.

16. How is *burglary* punished in whom ?   228.

———

CHAP. XVII.

Of Offences against private Property.

1. WHAT are the three offences against *private subjects*, which more immediately affect their *property*, two of which are attended with a *breach* of the *peace* ?   229.

2. Into what two sorts is *larciny*, by contraction for *laticony*, *latrocinium*, distinguished by the *law*?   229.

3. When is *simple larciny* called *grand*, and when *petit*, *larciny* ?   229.

4. What is *simple larciny* ?   229.

5. In what cases may a *carrier* of *goods* commit the *offence* of *larciny* upon those goods ? 230.

6. What is enacted by statutes 33 Hen. VI. c. 1., and 21 Hen. VIII. c. 7., in cases of *servants* embezzling their *master's goods* ?   230, 231.

7. What is the *offence* of embezzling goods, of which the offender had not the possession, but only the care or use ?   231.

8. Under what circumstances, may a man be guilty of *felony*, in taking his own *goods* ? 231.

9. What is a sufficient *asportation* of *goods*, to constitute a *larceny*? 231.

10. Who are indemnified by thé requisite to a *larciny*, that it must be *felonious*, that is, done *animo furandi*? 232.

11. Why can no *larciny* be committed, by the rules of *common law*, of things that adhere to the *freehold;* and why is the severance of them merely *trespass* by *common law;* but in what cases may the taking them away amount to *larciny*? 232, 233.

12. And now by statute 4 Geo. II. c. 32., how are what *offences* of this nature punished; and what is enacted by three statutes of Geo. III. as to the *offence* of stealing any trees, roots, shrubs, or plants ? 233, 234.

13. What instance of stealing out of *mines* is punished by statute 25 Geo. II. c. 10.; and how ? 234.

14. Why is it no *felony* to steal writings relating to a *real estate*? 234.

15. Upon what footing are *bonds*, *bills*, and *notes*, put by the statute 2 Geo. II c. 25.; and what is enacted as to embezzlements at the Bank of England, South Sea Company, and Post Office, by statutes 15 Geo. II. c. 13., 24 Geo. II. c. 11., and 7 Geo. III. c. 50.? 234, 235.

16. When may *larciny* be committed of *animals, feræ naturæ;* and what is enacted on this

subject by statutes 9 Geo. I. c. 22., 16 Geo. III.
c. 30., and 5 Geo. III. c, 14.? 23 , 23 .

17. Of what *animals domitiæ naturæ* can *larciny*
be committed; and what is enacted by
statute 10 Geo. III. c. 18., as to *dog-stealing?*
236.

18. Can *larciny* be committed, if the owner be
unknown ? 236.

19. When only is stealing a *corpse felony?* 236,
237.

20. How is *simple larciny.* whether *grand* or
petit, punished ; and how is the punishment
for the latter *offence* mitigated ? 238, 239.

21. But in what cases of *simple larciny*, is the
benefit of clergy taken away by statute ; and
why ? 239, 240.

22. What is *mixed*, or *compound larciny?* 240.

23. What is *larciny* from the *house ;* in what four
domestic aggravations of *larciny*, above the
value of twelve-pence, is the benefit of clergy
denied, and to whom, in what two *larcinies* to
the value of five shillings, and in what one to
the value of forty shillings ? 241, 242.

24. Of what two sorts is *larciny* from the *person?*
242.

25. How is the *offence* of privately stealing from
a man's *person* punished ? 242.

26. What three requisites are there to the *offence*
of open and violent *larciny* from the *person,*
or *robbery ;* and how, and in whom, is it now
in all cases punished ? 243, 244.

27. What is the *malicious mischief*, which the law considers as a *public crime*? 244.

28. What is enacted by statute 22 Hen. VIII. c. 11. as to destroying the powdike in the fens of Norfolk and Ely; what *offence* is it to destroy the sea-banks, river-banks, public navigations, and bridges, erected by virtue of many *acts* of *parliament*; what does the statute 43 Eliz. c. 13. enact, for preventing rapine on the northern borders, and what is *blackmail*; what is enacted by the statutes, 22 & 23 Car. II. c. 7., as to burning or destroying corn, hay, &c. or killing cattle; 4 & 5 W. & M. c. 23. as to burning on any waste, between Candlemas and Midsummer; 1 Ann. st. 2. c. 9., and 4 Geo. I. c. 12., as to destroying ships to the prejudice of the owners and insurers; 12 Ann. st. 2. c. 18. as to damaging ships in distress; 1 Geo. I. c. 46. as to setting on fire underwood; 6 Geo. I. c 23. as to defacing the garments of persons passing in the streets; by the *Waltham black-act*, extended to what by 9 Geo. III. c. 29.; by 6 Geo. II c. 37., and 10 Geo. II. c. 32, as to the cutting down banks, cutting hop-binds, or firing coal-mines; 11 Geo. II. c. 22. as to deterring buyers of corn, seizing corn-carriages or horses, or spoiling corn; 28 Geo. II. c. 19. as to firing furze in any forest or chase; 6 Geo. III. cc. 39. & 48., and 13 Geo. III.

c. 33., as to destroying trees or plants; 9 Geo. III. c. 29. as to the destroying mine-engines, or inclosure fences; and 13 Geo. III. c. 38. as to destroying the Plate-glass Company's property? 245—257.

29. What is *forgery*, or the *crimen falsi*? 247.

30. What *forgeries* have been capitally punished, by a multitude of statutes, since the *Revolution*, when paper-credit was first established? 248, 249.

31. What do several statutes of Geo. III enact as to *forgeries* of standard plate-marks, frauds on the *stamp-duties*, counterfeiting the Plate-glass Company's seal, and forging the superscription of a letter in order to avoid the payment of the postage? 249.; and see Mr. J. Christian's notes (7) and (8) to this page.

32. What is enacted by statute 2 Geo. II. c. 25. as to the *forgery* of deeds, wills, notes, &c.; and by statutes 7 Geo. II. c. 22., and 18 Geo. III. c. 18., as to acceptances of bills of exchange, or the number or principal sum of any accountable receipt for any security for money, or any order for the payment of money or the delivery of goods? 249, 250.

CHAP. XVIII.

Of the Means of Preventing Offences.

1. HOW may *crimes* and *misdemesnors* be prevented ? 251.
2. In what does this security consist ? 252, 253.
3. Who may demand it ; to whom may it be granted ; what is a writ called a *supplicavit ;* and how ought *feme-coverts* and *infants* to find security ? 253, 254.
4. In what four ways may a *recognizance* be discharged ? 254.
5. For what causes is a *recognizance* for the *peace* grantable ; what is called *swearing the peace* against another ; and what, if the party do not find such *sureties* as the *justice* shall require ? 254, 255.
6. How may such *recognizance* be forfeited ; when does a trespass upon the lands or goods of another, and when do mere reproachful words, forfeit such *recognizance ?* 255, 256.
7. Whom are the *justices* empowered by the statute 84 Edw. III. c. 1. to bind over to their *good abearance*, or *behaviour*, towards the *king* and his *people ;* who are holden to be comprised under the general words of this expression ; and what, if the *justice* commit a man for want of *sureties ?* 256.
8. How may such *recognizances* be forfeited ? 257.

CHAP. XIX.

Of Courts of a Criminal Jurisdiction.

1. IN discussing the method of inflicting punishments, what two things are to be considered ? 258.
2. Of what two natures are the several *courts* of *criminal jurisdiction?* 258.
3. In what degree are these *criminal courts* independent of each other ; and why are they so ; and which are the twelve *public* ones, ranking them, for this reason, according to their dignity ? 258, 259. 261. 265. 268, 269. 271. 273—275.
4. Who are tried by the *high court of parliament,* how, and for what *offences ;* and what is enacted by statute 12 & 13 W III. c 2. as to any *plea* of *pardon* under the *great seal?* 259—261.
5. For what is the *court* of the *lord high stewart* of *Great Britain* instituted ; how, and to whom is the office now granted ; what is the only *plea* a *peer* may *plead* in the *court* of *king's bench* ; what is the form of proceeding in case of a trial in the *court* of the *lord high steward ;* and what does the statute 7 W. III. c. 3. enact, as to the number of *peers* who shall vote on the *trial ?* 261—263.

6. Where is the trial of an indicted *peer* properly, during the *session of parliament;* and what different authority has the *lord high steward* when he sits in the *high court of parliament,* and when he sits in his own *court ?* 263.

7. Have *bishops* a right to sit in the *court* of the *lord high steward ;* and what do they, in point of fact *?* 264, 265.

8. What is the cognizance of the *crown side* of the *court of king's bench ;* and what is the effect of the coming of this *court* into any *county?* 265.

9. What was the *court* of *star-chamber,* and whither hath reverted all that was good and salutary of its jurisdiction ? 266, 267.

10. When was the *court of chivalry* a *criminal court;* and what used to be its jurisdiction then ? 268.

11. What *criminal* cognizance has the *court of admiralty ;* and what is the method of its *trials* by statutes 28 Hen. VIII. c. 15. ? 268, 269.

12. Before whom, and when, are the *courts* of *oyer* and *terminer,* and general *gaol-delivery,* held ? 269.

13. By virtue of what five several authorities, do the *judges* sit at what is usually called the *assizes,* two of which are of a *civil* nature, and have been before explained ? 269.

14. Who are bound to attend the third, which is the *commission* of the *peace ?* 270.

15. To whom are the fourth and fifth *commissions*

of *oyer* and *terminer*, and general *gaol-delivery*, directed; who are of the *quorum*, and what are they empowered to do? 270.

16. When are special commissions of *oyer* and *terminer* and *gaol-delivery*, issued? 271.

17. Can a man act as *judge*, or other *lawyer*, in these commissions, within his own *county*, where he was born, or has inhabited? 271.

18. When, and before whom, must the *court* of general *quarter sessions* of the *peace* be held, and what is its jurisdiction and mode of proceeding; is there any appeal from its *orders* upon *motion*; and who has the custody of its *records* or *rolls*? 271, 272.

19. What other *quarter sessions* are kept in most *corporation* towns; and in what one instance only have they, by statute 8 & 9 W. III. c. 30., the same authority, as the general *quarter sessions* of the *county*; and, for what purposes, in both *corporation towns* and *counties*, is a *special* or petty session held, by whom? 272, 273.

20. What is the *sheriff's tourn*, or *rotation* and when is it held? 273.

21. What is the *court leet*, or *view of frankpledge*; when, and before whom, is it held; whence is its origin; what is the jurisdiction of both the *sheriff's tourn* and this *court*; who are obliged to attend them; what has occasioned them to grow into disrepute; and where hath their business greatly devolved? 273, 274.

22. What is the object of the jurisdiction of the *court* of the *coroners?* 274.

23. To what is the *court* of the *clerk of the market* incident; what is the object of its jurisdiction; whence is the officer called the *clerk;* and what punishments has he authority to inflict? 275.

24. What are the three *private* or *special courts* of *criminal* jurisdiction? 276, 277.

25. For what purpose was the *court* of the *lord steward, treasurer,* or *comptroller* of the *king's household* instituted by statute 3 Hen. VII. c. 14.; and what is the course of its *proceedings?* 276.

26. For what purpose was the *court* of the *lord steward* of the *king's household,* or in his absence of the *treasurer, comptroller,* and *steward* of the *marshalsea,* erected by statute 33 Hen. VIII. c. 12.; and what is the course of its *proceedings?* 276.

27. What is the jurisdiction of the *criminal courts* of the two *universities,* or their *chancellors' courts;* what is the jurisdiction of the *court* of the *lord high steward* of the *university* (of Oxford, by charter of 7 June, 2 Hen. IV., confirmed by statute 13 Eliz. c. 29.); by whom must he be nominated and approved; and what is the course of proceeding, when any *indictment* is found against any person privileged by the *university?* 277, 278.

CHAP. XX.

Of Summary Convictions.

1. INTO what two kinds, are the *proceedings* in the *courts* of *criminal* jurisdiction divisible? 280.

2. What is meant by a *summary proceeding*; and what are the three branches of *summary proceedings*? 280—283.

3. By whom are all *trials* of *offences* and *frauds* contrary to the *laws* of *excise*, and other branches of the *revenue*, determined? 281.

4. What *offences* are punished in a *summary* way by *justices* of the *peace*; and to what three mischievous effects does the system give rise? 281, 282.

5. What is the process of these *summary convictions*; but what check has the *common law* thrown upon them, which is now held to be an absolute requisite to them? 282, 283.

6. Of what two sorts are the *contempts* which are immemorially punished in the *summary* way of *attachment* by the *superior courts* of *justice*? 283.

7. Of what seven kinds are the principal instances of either sort? 284, 285.

8. Why is the *attachment* for the species of *contempt*, arising from the disobedience to any *rule* or *order* of *court*, by *parties* to any

CHAP. XXI.

Of Arrests.

it be granted ; what is requisite to its legality ; what is a *special*, and what a *general warrant ;* and when, by statute 24 Geo. II. c. 44.,
is the *officer* who executes a *warrant* indemnified ?   290, 291.

4. Whither does a *warrant* from a *justice* of the
   court of *king's bench* extend, and where is it
   teste'd or *dated?*   291.

5. But what must take place, before the *warrant*
   of a *justice* of the *peace* in one *county,* can be
   executed in another ; and what is enacted on
   this subject by statute 13 Geo. III. c. 31. ?
   291, 292.

6. By what five *officers* may *arrests* be executed,
   without warrant ?   292.

7. When is any *private person* bound to make an
   arrest on what pain ; and what is he justified
   in doing, in order to such *arrest ;* but what, if
   the *arrest,* be only upon suspicion ?   293.

8. What is *arrest* by *hue* (from *huer,* to shout) and
   cry (hutesium et clamor) ; what does the statute of Winchester, 13 Edw. I. cc. 1. & 4.,
   direct, relative to this matter ; what is the
   foundation of an *action* against the *hundred,* in
   case of any loss by *robbery ;* what does the statute 27 Eliz. c. 13. enact, as to the sufficiency
   of *hue and cry,* and what that of Geo. II. c. 16.
   if an *officer* refuse or neglect to make it ; by
   whom may it be raised ; what powers has the
   constable in its prosecution ; and what, if it be

wantonly and maliciously raised without cause? 223 294.

9. What rewards and immunities are bestowed on such as apprehend *felons*, by statutes 4 & 5 W. & M. c. 8. and 8 Geo. II. c. 16., as to *highwaymen;* by statutes 6 & 7 W. III. c. 17., and 15 Geo. II. c. 28., as to *offenders* against the *coinage;* by statutes 10 & 11 W. III. c. 23., and 5 Ann. c. 31., as to *burglars;* by statute 6 Geo. I. c. 23., as to helpers of others to their stolen goods, for reward; by statutes 14 Geo. II. c. 6. and 15 Geo. II. c. 34., as to sheep-stealers; and by statutes 16 Geo. II. c. 15. and 8 Geo. III. c. 15., as to premature returners from transportation? 295.

———

CHAP. XXII.

Of Commitment and Bail.

1. WHAT is the *justice,* before whom a *prisoner* is brought, bound to do by statute 2 & 3 Ph. & M. c. 10.; and in what cases only is it lawful totally to discharge him? 296.

2. When must he be *committed* to prison; and when ought *bail* to be taken? 296, 297.

3. What *offence* is it by the *common law,* as well as by the statute Westm. 1. and the *habeas*

corpus act, to refuse or delay to *bail* any person *bailable* ; and what is expressly declared, as to *excessive bail*, by statute 1 W. & M. st. 2. c. 1. ?   297.

4. On the other hand, what if the *magistrate* take insufficient *bail?*   297.

5. Upon what ten accusations are persons clearly not admissible to *bail* by the *justices?*   298, 299.

6. Upon what three accusations do persons seem to be in the discretion of the *justices*, whether bailable or not?   299.

7. Upon what three accusations, *must* persons be *bailed*, upon offering sufficient security ? 299.

8. But who may *bail* for any *crime* whatsoever, except only persons committed by whom? 299, 300.

9. This imprisonment being only for safe custody, what is the *gaoler* not justified in doing ?   300.

CHAP. XXIII.

Of the several Modes of Prosecution.

1. IN what two ways are *offenders prosecuted*, or formally accused?   301.

2. By one of what two *proceedings* is the former way of *prosecution?*   301.

3. What is a *presentment*, properly speaking ? 301.

4. What is an *inquisition of office,* and of what two kinds ? 301, 302.
5. What is an *indictment* ? 302.
6. Of whom are the *grand jury* composed ; by whom are they instructed, or *charged;* and what *evidence* only are they to hear ? 302, 303.
7. In what case only can the *grand jury* inquire of a fact, done out of that *county,* for which they are sworn ; and what is enacted by the statute 2 & 3 Edw. VI. c. 24., when a man is wounded in one *county* and dies in another ; by statute 2 Geo. II. c. 21., if the stroke or poisoning be in England, and the death out of it, or *vice versâ;* by several statutes of Hen. VIII. and Edw. VI. where *treason* is committed out of the realm; by two statutes of Hen. VIII., as to *offences* against the *coinage,* committed in Wales; by statute 33 Hen. VIII. c. 23., as to *trials* for *murder* by the *King's special commission ;* by statute 10 & 11 W. III. c. 25., as to *capital crimes* committed in *Newfoundland;* by statute 9 Geo. I. c. 22., as to *offences* against the *black act;* by stats. 8 Geo. II. c. 20. and 13 Geo. III. c. 84., as to *felonies* in destroying *turnpikes* or *river-works ;* by statute 26 Geo. II. c. 19., as to stealing from *vessels wrecked,* or in *distress;* by statute 12 Geo. III. c. 24., as to destroying the *King's ships* out of this realm; and by sta-

tute 13 Geo. III. c. 63., as to *misdemesnors* committed in India ? 303—305.

8. In what cases, is the *offence* to complete in two *counties* or parts of the *kingdom*, that the offender may be *indicted* in either ? 305.

6. What do the *grand jury*, if, having heard the *evidence*, they think the accusation groundless ; may a fresh *bill* be preferred ; and what do they, if they be satisfied of the truth of the accusation ? 305.

10. But what number of the *grand jury* must agree, in order to *find* a *bill?* 306.

11. What three things must be precisely and sufficiently ascertained in an *indictment?* 306.

12. What is enacted by statute 1 Hen. V. c. 5., as to the identification of the *person;* in what case is a mistake in the *time* and *place* not held to be material ; but when is it very material that the *indictment* should name the *time* ? 306.

13. In what *crimes* must particular words of art be used, which are so appropriated by *law* to express the precise ideas which it entertains of the *offence*, that no other words, however synonymous they may seem, are capable of doing it ? 307.

14. In what cases, in *indictments* for *murder*, need not the length and depth of the *wound* be expressed ; and when is it necessary that the thing, which is the subject or instrument of the *offence*, should be expressed ? 307.

15. By one of what two *proceedings* is the method of *prosecution*, without any previous *finding* by a *jury ?* 308, 312.

16. What was the proceeding when a *thief* was taken with the *mainour ;* and when does a similar *process* remain to this day ? 307, 308.

17. Of what two sorts are *informations ;* and what are the limitations of *prosecutions* upon *penal statutes*, by statute 31 Eliz. c. 5. ? 308.

18. Of what two kinds are the *informations* which are exhibited in the name of the *King* alone ; by whom are they respectively *filed ;* what are their respective objects ; and by whom must they be *tried*, and by whom punished ? 308, 309.

19. But to what are these *informations* confined ? 310.

20. What is enacted by statute 4 & 5 W. & M. c. 18., as to *informations* exhibited by the *master* of the *crown-office ;* but what as to *informations* at the *King's* own *suit*, filed by the *attorney-general ?* 311, 312.

21. Is there not still another species of *information ?* 312.

22. What is the method of *criminal prosecution*, which is merely at the *suit* of the *subject* by *appeal ;* and why has it falllen into disuse ? 312, 313.

23. What is the origin of an *appeal ;* and what was a *weregild ?* 313, 314.

24. What are the only two *appeals* now in force ?
314.

25. For what *crimes* against the *parties* themselves, may *appeals* be instituted ; what is the
only *crime* against one's *relation*, for which an
appeal can be brought ; and by what *relations*
only can this be brought ?　314.

26. What, if the *wife* marry again, before, pending, or after, *judgment* of her *appeal;* when
shall the *heir*, and when shall the *wife* not
have the *appeal;* what, if there be no *wife*,
and the *heir* be accused of the *murder ;* and
within what time, by the statute of Gloucester,
must all *appeals* of *death* be sued ? 314, 315.

27. If the *apellee* be acquitted, can he be afterwards *indicted* for the same *offence ;* and if a
man be acquitted on an *indictment* of *murder*,
or *found guilty*, and pardoned by the *King*,
what, in strictness, ought to happen, by virtue
of the statute 3 Hen. VII. c. 1. ; but what, if
he have been *found guilty* of *manslaughter* on
an *indictment*, and have had the *benefit of clergy*, and suffered the *judgment* of the *law ?* 315.

28. What shall the *appellor* suffer, by virtue of the
statute of Westm. 2., if the *appellee* be acquitted ?　316.

29. If the *appellee* be *found guilty*, what *judgment*
shall he suffer, with what remarkable difference from the consequences of a *conviction*
by *indictment* ?　316.

CHAP. XXIV.

Of Process upon an Indictment.

1. IF the *offender* have fled, or secrete himself in *capital* cases, or have not, in smaller *misdemesnors*, been bound over to appear at the *assises* or *sessions* may an *indictment* be preferred against him in his absence ; can he be tried, although he do not personally appear ; and what is the express provision of statute 28 Edw. III. c. 3. ? 318.

2. What is the proper *process* to bring in an *offender*, or an *indictment* for any *petty misdemesnor*, or on a *penal statute ?* 318.

3. What, if, by the *return* to such *process*, it appear that the *party* hath *lands* in the *county ;* and what, if the *sheriff* return, that he hath none in his *bailiwick ?* 318, 319.

4. But what happens, on *indictments* for *treason* or *felony ;* and what is now the usual practice in the case of *misdemesnors ?* 319.

5. When shall the *offender* be put in *exigent*, in order to his *outlawry ;* and what is the form and consequence of this *proceeding ?* 319.

6. What is the punishment for *outlawries* upon *indictments* for *misdemesnors ;* but to what does an *outlawry* in *treason* or *felony* amount ? 319.

7. Who may arrest an *outlaw*, on a *criminal pro-escution*; and when is the whole *outlawry* illegal, and may be reversed? 320.

8. When may a *writ* of *certiorari facias* be had; what is its effect; and for what four purposes is this frequently done? 320, 321.

9. At whose instance may a *certiorari* be granted; and when is it generally refused? 321.

10. When, and how, must *indictments found* by the *grand jury* against a *peer*, or in places of exclusive jurisdiction, be delivered into the *court* of *parliament*, or into that of the *lord high steward*, or to the courts of such exclusive jurisdiction! 321.

CHAP. XXV.

Of Arraignment, and its Incidents.

1. WHAT is *arraignment (ad rationem ponere,* in French, *ad reson*, or abbreviated, *à resn)?* 322.

2. Why is the *prisoner* called upon to hold up his hand; and what, if he refuse to do so? 323.

3. In what cases, by statute 1 Ann. c. 9., may the *accessory* be proceeded against, as if the *principal felon* had been attainted; and why? 324.

4. One of what two circumstances is *incident* to every *arraignment?* 324.

5. In what three cases, is a *prisoner* said to *stand mute?* 324.

6. What ought the *court* to do, if the *prisoner* say nothing; and what, if he appear to be *dumb ex visitatione Dei*, in which case, can *judgment* of death be given against him ?   324, 325.

7. But what hath long been clearly settled, if he be *found* to be *obstinately mute* in *high treason, petit larceny,* and all *misdemesnors;* and what, by the antient law, in *appeals* or *indictments* for other *felonies* or *petit treason ?*   325.

8. What was *trina admonitio ;* was the *benefit of clergy* allowed to an *obstinate mute;* and what was the *sentence* of *penance* or *peine (prisone) forte et dure ?*   325. 327.

9. Was the *trial by rack* ever attempted to be introduced into England ?   326.

10. To what did *standing mute* amount, in all cases, by the *common law ;* did the *prisoner* derive any advantage from suffering *death* by the *sentence* of *peine forte et dure*, over that of *judgment* upon *trial;* and what was enacted in abolition of this *sentence*, by statute 12 Geo. III. c. 20. ?   328, 329.

11. What is the consequence of the *prisoner's simple confession* of the *indictment ?*   329.

12. But what is confession by way of *approvement;* who is the *approver* or *prover, probator*, and who the *appellee ;* in what *offences* only can an *approvement* be ; to what does

it amount ; and what, if the *appellee* be acquitted ? 329, 330.

13. Why has the admission of *approvements* been
long disused by *courts of justice ;* and how is
all the good arising from the method of *approvements* provided for, by several statutes,
in the cases of *coining, robbery, burglary,
house-breaking, horse-stealing,* and *larceny* to
the value of 5s. from *shops, stables,* &c. and
by statute 29 Geo. II. c. 30. in case of *metal-
stealing ?* 330, 331.

14. What is the usual practice, too, of *justices of
the peace,* as to admitting what is generally
termed *King's evidence?* 331.

CHAP. XXVI.

Of Plea, and Issue.

1. WHAT is the *plea* of the *prisoner ;* in what
cases does he *plead ;* and of what five kinds
is the *plea ?* 332.

2. What was the *plea of sanctuary ;* when might
a *criminal* claim *sanctuary ;* what did it su-
perinduce ; and when was the whole privilege
abolished ? 332, 333.

3. Was there not another *declinatory plea,* which
was used to be *pleaded* before *trial* or *conviction ?* 333.

4. What is a *plea* to the *jurisdiction* ; and when may it be made ? 333.

5. When is a *demurrer* to the *indictment* incident to *criminal* cases ; what, if the point of *law* be adjudged against the *prisoner ;* and why are *demurrers* to *indictments* seldom used ? 333, 334.

7. For what principally is a *plea* in *abatement ;* but why, in the end, does little advantage accrue to the *prisoner,* by means of these dilatory *pleas ?* 334, 335.

7. What are *special pleas* in *bar ;* of what four kinds, as applicable to both *appeals* and *indictments ?* 335.

8. Upon what universal maxim of the *common law,* is the *plea* of *autrefoits acquit* grounded ; is an *acquittal* on an *appeal* a good bar to an *indictment* on the same *offence,* and *vice ver-sâ,* taking into consideration what was enacted by the statute 3 Hen. VII. c. 1., to prevent the practice of not trying any person on an *indictment* of *homicide,* till after the year and day, within which *appeals* may be brought, were past, by which time it often happened, that the *witnesses* died, or the whole was forgotten ? 335, 336.

9. When, and of what, is the *plea* of *autrefoits, convict* a good *plea* in *bar ?* 336.

10. Of what is the *plea* of *autrefoits attaint* a good *plea* in *bar ;* and wherefore does it differ from the former two *pleas ?* 336.

11. But what four exceptions are there to this general rule, wherein, *cessante ratione, cessat et ipsa lex ;* and from these instances, what invariable requisite to the validity of a *plea* of *autrefois attaint* may we collect ?   336, 337.

12. What is one advantage that attends *pleading* a *pardon* in *bar* or in *arrest* of *judgment* before *sentence* is past, which gives it by much the preference to *pleading* it after *sentence* or *attainder?*   337.

13. Wherein do *special pleas* in *bar* differ in *criminal prosecutions*, and in *civil actions*, and why ; and when a *prisoner's plea* in *bar* is *found* or *adjudged* against him, what shall he have; for what is the only *plea* in consequence whereof *death* can be inflicted ?   338.

14. In cases of what *indictments* can there be no *special justification* put in, by way of *plea*, and why ; and why is the *general issue not guilty*, *non culpabilis* or *nient culpable*, the most advantageous *plea* for a *prisoner?*   338, 339.

15. How does the commentator explain the abbreviations of " *non cul.*," which was formerly used to be written upon the *minutes*, when the *prisoner* had *pleaded not guilty*, and " *cul. prit.*," the *replication* on behalf of the *King*, by which *issue* was joined, and which, from the circumstances of the *clerk of the arraigns* immediately inquiring of the prisoner, " *cul. prit.* how wilt thou be tried ?"

is commonly understood, as if he had fixed an opprobrious name on the prisoner? 339, 340.

16. But what is Mr. J. Christian's conjecture, as to the word *prit?* See his note (1) to this chapter.

17. To what only has this form of inquiry reference at present ; what can be the only *trial* upon *indictments*, since the abolition of *ordeal* and, therefore, what, if the *prisoner* refuse to put himself upon the *inquest* in the usual form? 340, 341.

18. When the *prisoner* has put himself upon his *trial*, (and in what words is this done?) what does the *clerk* answer? 341.

CHAP. XXVII.

Of Trial and Conviction.

1. WHAT was *trial* by *ordeal;* of what two sorts; and what, when they were performed by *deputy?* 342, 343.

2. How was *fire-ordeal* performed? 343.

3. How was *water-ordeal;* and in what practice may relics of it be traced? 343.

4. How was this *trial* abolished? 345.

5. What was *trial* by the *corsned?* 345.

6. In what *criminal* cases may the *trial* by *battel* be demanded ; what is the difference between

this *trial*, on a *writ of right*, and on these *cri-minal* cases ; and therefore who may *counter-plead* and refuse the *wager* of *battel*, and compel the other *party* to put himself upon the *country*, and when may the *crime* itself be sufficient cause of such refusal ?   3·16, 347.

7. Wherein do the *oaths* of the two *combatants* differ in *waging battel* upon *appeals*, and upon *writs of right?*   347, 348.

8. When shall a *peer* be tried by the *court of parliament* or the *lord high steward*, and when by a *jury ;* and in what two things only, does the *trial* by these *courts* differ from the *trial per patriam*, or *by jury?*   348., see Mr. J. Christian's note (2) at this page, and 349.

9. What is the *sheriff*'s duty when a *prisoner*, on his *arraignment*, has *pleaded not guilty*, and, for his *trial*, hath put himself upon the *country*, which *country* the *jury* are ; what, if the *proceedings* are before the *court of King's bench*, and then where is the *trial* had ; and what, before *commissioners* of *oyer and terminer* and *gaol delivery?*   3·0, 351.

10. What is customary, when persons *indicted* of smaller *misdemesnors* have *pleaded not guilty*, or *traversed* the *indictment?*   351.

11. In cases of *high treason* (except in counterfeiting the *King's coin* or *seals*, as much of the latter *act*, as relates to which, is repealed by statute 16 Geo. III. c. 53.), or *misprision*

of treason, what is enacted by statutes 7.
W. III. c. 3. and 7 Ann. c. 21. ? 351, 352.

12. By whom, and what kind, may *challenges*
of *jurors* be made, when the *trial* is called
on ? 352.

13. What are *challenges for cause*; and in *criminal*, or at least in *capital*, cases, what other
species of *challenge* is allowed to the *prisoner*, and for what two reasons ? 353.

14. What is enacted as to the denial of this privilege to the *King*, by statute 33 Edw. I.
st. 4. ? 353.

15. But what is the boundary of the *prisoner's
peremptory challenges* by the *common law*; and
how does it deal with one who *peremptorily*
challenges beyond that boundary ? 354.

16. But by statute 22 Hen. VIII. c. 14. how
many *peremptory challenges* can any person
arraigned for *felony* be permitted to make;
and what, if the *prisoner* challenge more
than that number ? 354.

17. May a *tales* be awarded in *criminal prosecutions*? 354, 355.

18. What is done when the *jury* is sworn, if it be
a *cause* of any consequence; but when only
shall *counsel* be allowed a *prisoner* upon his
trial, upon the *general issue*, in any *capital
crime*, and upon what principle ? 355.

19. But for what purpose, do the *judges* never
scruple to allow a *prisoner counsel*; and what
is directed by statute 7 W. III. c. 3., and

20 Geo. II. c. 30., lest this indulgence should be intercepted by superior influence, in the case of *state criminals?*   355, 356.

20. In what five leading points, by several statutes and resolutions, has a difference been made between *civil* and *criminal evidence?* 356. 358, 359.

21. What hath been holden in the construction of the statute 7 W. III. c. 3., by which it is enacted, that the *confession* of the *prisoner*, which shall countervail the necessity of proof of *treasons* by two *witnesses*, must be in *open court?*   357.

22. What two rules does Sir Matthew Hale lay down, as to admitting presumptive *evidence* cautiously?   359.

23. What was declared by statute 1 Ann. st. 2. c. 9., as to *witnesses* for the *prisoner?*   360.

24. What is the difference between the *verdict* in *civil* and *criminal* cases?   360.

25. What, if the *verdict* be notoriously wrong; and what hath been done, in many instances, where, contrary to *evidence*, the *jury* have found the *prisoner guilty?*   361.

26. What, if the *jury find* the *prisoner not guilty;* but what is he said to be, if the *jury find* him *guilty?*   361, 362.

27. In what two ways may *conviction* accrue? 362.

28. When shall the *prosecutor* be allowed the expences of *prosecution*, and a compensation for

his trouble and loss of time, out of what; and when shall all persons appearing upon *recognizance*, or *subpœna*, to give *evidence*, be paid their *charges*, and an allowance for their trouble and loss of time, by several late statutes ? 362.

29. When shall the *prosecutor* have restitution of his *goods*, by statute 21 Hen. VIII. c. 11., out of what, and by what *process* ? 362, 363.

30. Why does this *writ* of *restitution* reach the stolen *goods*, notwithstanding they have been sold to a third person in *market-overt ;* when may the *party* robbed regain the *goods*, without such *writ* of *restitution ;* and what, if the *felon* be *convicted* and *pardoned*, or be allowed his *clergy ?* 363.

31. When, and why, does the *court* permit the *de--fendant* to *speak with the prosecutor* before *judgment*, and, if the prosecutor then declare himself satisfied, inflict but a trivial punishment ; but when should this practice never be suffered, and why ? 363, 364.

CHAP. XXVIII.

Of the Benefit of Clergy.

1. AFTER trial and conviction, what is the principal intervening circumstance that suspends or arrests *judgment* ? 365.

2. In what had *clergy*, the *privilegium clericale*, or, in common speech, the *benefit of clergy*, its original ; and of what two principal kinds were the exemptions which were granted to the *church ?* 365.

3. When was it finally settled in the reign of Henry VI. that the *prisoner* might claim his benefit of *clergy ?* 366.

4. In process of time, who was accounted a *clerk*, or *cleric*, and what distinction was therefore drawn by statute 4 Hen. VII. c. 13., and virtually restored, after a temporary abolition by two statutes of Hen. VIII., by statute 1 Edw. VI. c. 12., which enacted what ? 367.

5. What became of the *offenders*, after they had had the benefit of their *clergy*, and were discharged from the sentence of the *law* in the *King's courts ?* 368.

6. But what happened, when upon very heinous and notorious circumstances of guilt, the *temporal courts* delivered over to the *ordinary*, the *convicted clerk, absque purgatione facienda ?* 369.

7. For avoiding these *perjuries* and abuses, what does the statute 18 Eliz. c. 7. enact ; and how long did the law continue thus, altered only, by an indulgence to whom, of the benefit of *clergy*, without the test ? 369, 370.

8. What was enacted by statute 5 Ann. c. 6., upon the considerations that learning was no extenuation of guilt, and that the lenity

of *clergy* was an encouragement to commit
the lower degrees of *felony*; in what cases
did the statutes 4 Geo. I. c. 11. and 6 Geo. I.
c. 23. give the *court* a discretionary power,
to commit the penalties of *burning in the
hand* or *whipping*, for *transportation* for seven
years? 370.

9. But now, by statute 19 Geo. III. c. 74. for
what have the *judges* a discretionary power
to commute the penalty of *transportation*;
(with what exception?) what if the *offenders*
escape a first, and what if a second time;
and for what (with what exceptions?) may
the *court* commute the penalty of *burning in
the hand?* 370, 371.

10. To what persons, is the benefit of *clergy* to be
allowed at this day? 371, 372.

11. For what *crimes* is the benefit of *clergy* to be
allowed? 372, 373.

12. What is declared by statute 28 Hen. VIII.
c. 15. as to the allowance of the benefit of *clergy* in the *marine law?* 373.

13. Unless what, is *clergy* now allowable in all
felonies, whether new created, or by *common
law?* 373.

14. Where *clergy* is taken away from the *principal*, is it from the *accessory?* 373.

15. Where *clergy* is taken away from the *offence*,
is a principal in the second degree excluded
from his *clergy?* 373.

16. Where it is taken away only from the *person*

CHAP. XXIX.

Of Judgment and its Consequences.

5. What if all *motions* in *arrest* of *judgment* fail ?
376.

6. Of what parts of *capital judgments* has the humanity of the English nation authorised an
almost general mitigation ? 376, 377.

7. How far is the punishment for every *offence*
ascertained by our English law ? 377, 378.

8. What has the *bill of rights* declared as to *fines*
and *punishments* ? 378, 379.

9. What has *magna carta*, c. 14., determined concerning *amercements* for misbehaviour by
the *suitors* in matters of *civil right;* and
what has it directed in order to ascertain this
amercement ? 379.

10. Who were *affeerors;* what is the difference
between an *amercement* and a *fine;* what is
the reason why *fines* in the *King's courts*
are frequently denominated *ransoms;* and
what is holden where any statute speaks
both of *fine* and *ransom* ? 379, 380.

11. Upon *judgment* of either of what two things,
on a *capital crime*, shall a man be said to be
attainted (attinctus, stained or *blackened)* ?
380. 381.

12. What are the incapacities of a man *attaint* ?
380.

13. What is the great difference between a man
convicted and *attainted* ? 381.

14. What are the two consequences of *attainder* ?
381.

15. How is *forfeiture* two-fold? 381.
16. How far backwards does *forfeiture* of *real estates* relate? 381.
17. What is forfeited from the *wife*, if the *husband* be *attainted* of *treason*, by the express provision of statute 5 & 6 Edw. VI. c. 11.; and if the *wife* be so, shall the *husband* be *tenant by the curtesy* of the *wife's land*? 381, 382.
18. But what if a *traitor* die before *judgment* pronounced, or be killed in open rebellion, or hanged by *martial law*? 382.
19. In what consideration, is the natural justice of *forfeiture*, or *confiscation* of *property*, founded? 382.
20. What is provided in certain *treasons* relating to the *coin;* and in order to abolish hereditary punishment entirely, what was enacted by statute 7 Ann. c. 21., and how was the operation of the indemnifying clauses in this statute still farther suspended by statute 17 Geo. II. c. 39.? 384, 385.
21. What does the *offender* forfeit, in *petit treason* and *felony;* and what is called the *King's year, day,* and *waste?* 385.
22. Do these *forfeitures* actually take place; are they incident to a *felo de se;* and how far backwards do they relate? 386.
23. To what two other instances, besides those already spoken of, does the *forfeiture* of the profits of *land* during life extend? 386.

CHAP. XXX.

Of reversal of Judgment.

2. By what three means, may a *judgment* and *attainder* be reversed ? 390—39ぇ.

3. For what may a *judgment* be falsified, reversed. or avoided, *without a writ of error ;* why cannot these matters be assigned for *error* in the *superior court ;* and when may a *diminution* of the *record* be alleged ? 390.

4. Where does a *writ of error* lie, and for what may it be brought ? 391, 392.

5. On what are *writs of error* allowed to reverse *judgments* in case of *misdemesnors ;* and how in *capital cases* to reverse attainders, when by whom are they generally brought ? 392.

6. When is an *act* of *parliament* to reverse the *attainder* granted, and how is its effect different from that of a reversal by *writ of error ?* 392.

7. What is the effect of falsifying, or reversing, an *outlawry ;* and wherein does it differ from that of falsifying, or reversing, a *judgment* upon *conviction ?* 392, 393.

8. Upon the latter event taking place, what if the *party's estates* have been granted away by the *crown ?* 393.

9. Is he liable to another prosecution for the same *offence ?* 393.

CHAP. XXXI.

Of Reprieve and Pardon.

1. WHAT is a *reprieve*, from *reprendre*, to *take back*; and on what two accounts may it be? 394.

2. What is a *reprieve ex arbitrio judicis*, and when may it be granted or taken off? 394.

3. What is the first case of *reprieve* granted *ex necessitate legis*; and what must the *judge* direct in case the *plea* of *pregnancy*, in a *woman capitally convicted*, be made in stay of *execution*; when is it a sufficient stay; and how long? 395.

4. What if the *woman* have once had the benefit of this *reprieve*, and been delivered, and afterwards become pregnant again? 395.

5. What is the second cause of regular *reprieve*? 395, 396.

6. What is it the invariable rule to demand of the *prisoner*, when any time intervenes between the *attainder* and the award of *execution*; and what if the party plead *diversity* of *person*, that he is not the same that was *attainted*, and the like? 396.

7. When only, in these collateral *issues*, shall time be allowed the *prisoner* to make his *defence*, or produce his *witnesses*; and what is held as to *challenges* of the *jury* by the *prisoner*? 396.

37

8. What is declared by statute 27 Hen. VIII.
c. 24., as to *pardon?* 397.

9. What *offences* may the *king* pardon, excepting
what four? 398, 399.

10. What restriction is there, that affects the prerogative of pardoning, in case of *parliamen-*
tary impeachments? 399, 400.

11. What must be the *form* of a complete irre-
vocable *pardon;* and what will be the effect
of a *warrant* under the *privy seal* or *sign*
manual? 400.

12. What circumstance will vitiate the whole
pardon? 400.

13. Will a *pardon* of *all felonies* pardon a *convic-*
tion or *attainder* of *felony?* 400.

14. What is enacted by the statute 13 Ric. II.
st. 2. c. 1., as to the *pardon* of *treason, mur-*
der, or *rape?* 400.

15. Under these restrictions, how is it a general
rule that a *pardon* shall be taken? 401.

16. What is a *conditional pardon?* 401.

17. What is the difference between a *pardon* by
act of *parliament,* and by the *king's charter*
of *pardon?* 402.

18. When has a man waived the benefit of his
pardon? 402.

19. What discretionary power does the statute
5 & 6 W. & M. c. 13. give the *judges* of the
court over a *criminal pleading pardon* of
felony? 402.

20. What is the effect of a *pardon* by the *king?*
402.

21. But what only can restore or purify the
blood, if the *pardon* be not allowed till after
attainder; yet when may the *attainted's son*
be his *heir?*   402.

CHAP. XXXII.

Of Execution.

1. BY whom must *execution* be performed ; and
under what *warrant* in the *court* of the *lord
high steward,* under what in the *court* of the
peers in *parliament,* and under what at the
assises?   403.

2. Within what time is the *sheriff* to do *execution,*
in the country ; but what is the form of proceeding, and what is the *warrant* in *London,*
and what if the *prisoner* be *tried* at the *bar*
of, or brought by *habeas corpus* into, the
court of *king's bench?*   404.

3. And throughout the kingdom, what is enacted
by 25 Geo. II. c. 37., in case of *murder?* 404.

4. Can the *sheriff* alter the manner of the execution, by substituting one *death* for another ?
404.

5. May the *king,* or may he, remit any part of
the *sentence?*   405.

6. What if, upon execution of judgment to be hanged by the neck till he is dead, the *criminal* revives ? 406.

CHAP. XXXIII.

Of the Rise, Progress, and gradual Improvements, of the Laws of England.

1. What few points, which bear a great affinity and resemblance to some of the modern doctrines of our English law, may be collected from Cæsar's account of the tenets and discipline of the ancient Druids in Gauls, who were sent over to Britain to be instructed? 408.

2. Why is it impossible to trace out *when* the several mutations of the *common law* were made ; and whence the great variety of our ancient established customs ? 408—410.

3. What did Alfred for the *constitution* and *laws ?* 410, 411.

4. What was the *Dane-lage*, what the *West-Saxon-lage*, and what the *Mercen-lage ?* 412.

5. What did Edgar ; and what is the most probable original of the *common law ?* 412.

6. What nine may be reckoned among the most remarkable of the Saxon laws ? 412—414.

7. What five alterations in our *laws* did the Norman invasion work ? 415—418.

8. What did William Rufus; and what did Henry I. ? 420, 421.
9. What did Stephen? 421.
10. What did Henry II.; and what four things peculiarly merit the attention of the legal antiquary in the reign of this *king* ? 421 —423.
11. What did Richard I. ? 423.
12. What did John and Henry III.; and what were the effects of *magna carta* and *carta de foresta?* 423—425.
13. What did Edward I.; to what principal fifteen general heads may the regulations of this *king* be reduced; and what is the best proof of the excellence of his constitutions? 425—427.
14. What did Edwards II. and III. ? 428.
15. What was done from this time to that of Henry VII.; and what two things do we owe to the *civil wars* and disputed titles to the crown? 428, 429.
16. What was done by Henry VII. ? 429, 430.
17. What did the *reformation* effect; and what was done with regard also to our *civil* polity by Henry VIII. ? 430, 431.
18. What did Edward VI. and Mary? 431, 432.
19. What did Elizabeth for the religious liberties of the nation; and what for the political? 432—435.

20. What did James I.?   436.

21. What did Charles I.?   436—438.

22. What was done, upon the *restoration* of Charles II.?   438—440.

23. What has been done from the *revolution* in 1688 to the present time; and what have been the chief alterations of moment in the administration of private justice, during that period?   440, 442.

THE END.

Printed in the United States
45280LVS00004B/90

9 781417 953011